BLAIR HUGHES-STANTON

THE WOOD-ENGRAVINGS OF

BLAIR

HUGHES-STANTON

PENELOPE

HUGHES-STANTON

PRIVATE LIBRARIES ASSOCIATION

PINNER

Published by the Private Libraries Association
Ravelston, South View Road, Pinner,
Middlesex HA5 3YD, England

1750 copies (of which 600 for sale)
SBN 900002 75 1
112 copies with eight engravings
printed, from the wood, by I. M. Imprimit
SBN 900002 85 9
A CIP catalogue record for this book is
available from the British Library

Printed in Great Britain by
W. S. Maney & Son Ltd
Hudson Road, Leeds LS9 7DL
Bound by The Fine Bindery

Designed by
David Chambers

CONTENTS

ILLUSTRATIONS

Reproductions are full size unless noted otherwise in the caption.
◀ by an illustration indicates that it is placed on its side, its lower edge to the right.

BLAIR HUGHES-STANTON

Hughes-Stanton is probably the most remarkable engraver in the country: in the world perhaps. His stimulus usually comes from literary subject-matter, but once the associations start working in his mind, they are almost immediately visualised in terms of box-wood and engraved textures. I have seen him make the merest scribble on the surface of the blackened design, from start to finish on the block, without a break in contemplating and handling the wood and the tools. This sensuousness of approach to the medium sometimes possessed him, so that he worked at great speed leaving a trail of textures like that of a comet beyond the actual forms and shapes associated with the subject. He was an expressionist. But to find an expressionist who is able to take an intractible medium like wood-engraving and make it a flexible instrument for his fancy and sensuous flights is unique. His actual hands were tireless: they seemed to gain energy from contact with the wood and the graver. It looked as though his mental associations were shaped by the medium before they even reached his consciousness.

WILLIAM McCANCE

from 'The Wood-Engravings of Blair Hughes-Stanton', by John Lewis, *Image*, 6, Spring 1951.

PREFACE

This book is intended as an introduction to the life and work of my father, Blair Hughes-Stanton, with special reference to his wood-engravings. These have hitherto been known only to a narrow public, largely because the majority appeared in private press books of limited circulation and because the few dozen of his personal independent engravings were printed in small editions. Although reproductions of BHS's work have appeared in most publications concerned with the history of British wood-engraving, they have never been reproduced in any great number or logical sequence. Moreover the extent to which BHS pushed the medium to its limits (some say beyond), and the consequent problems of achieving the density of the black areas while retaining the extreme delicacy of the fine engraved white lines, have always conspired against adequate reproduction. The plates in this book are as good as present technology allows.

The representative selection of engravings is preceded by a detailed checklist of the books containing illustrations by BHS and a list of his independent prints including the later linocuts. I have attempted to keep the introductory biographical section as concise and as relevant to the work as possible.

The use throughout the text of my father's initials, rather than of his Christian name or our cumbersome surname, was adopted partly for brevity and convenience and partly for a distance which would enable me to be more objective than might be expected from a devoted daughter. In quoting BHS's own (largely unpunctuated) writings and Paul Collet's transcription of his tape-recorded musings, I have sometimes taken the liberty of adding punctuation for the sake of clarity.

There are many people without whose help and encouragement this book would never have been completed. Thanks go first to Ian Mortimer who mentioned the idea to my father and me many years ago and who suggested David Chambers and the Private Libraries Association as publisher. I am deeply grateful to David Chambers himself for his unfailing enthusiasm, knowledge and patience, all of which spurred me on in the intervals between unavoidable distractions; to Dorothy Harrop, Kathleen Ladizesky, Paul Collet and James Hamilton on whose scholarship I have drawn and to all the other authors from whose works I have quoted; to Arthur Calder-Marshall, Rodney Thomas, Sir Robert Sainsbury, the late Lady Sainsbury, Lewis Allen and especially to Ida

Graves without whose contributions the writing and the result would have been dull indeed; to Professor Jim Boulton of Birmingham University, who drew my attention to relevant letters from D. H. Lawrence, and to Laurence Pollinger Ltd. and the Estate of Mrs Frieda Lawrence Ravagli who permitted me to use them; to my mother, Anne Hughes-Stanton, and my half-sisters, Judith Russell and Kristin Baybars, who provided crucial material and checked the manuscript; to my friends Anna Merton, Griselda Musset, Selwyn Image, David Esslemont, and Antony Griffiths who read the manuscript and made valuable comments; to Terry Sole for elusive bibliographical details and frequent enquiries as to completion; and finally to Norman Ackroyd, whose continuous encouragement I cannot begin to quantify. All mistakes, inaccuracies and omissions are of course entirely my own.

We acknowledge with thanks permission from the following to reproduce from their books: the Trustees of the Seven Pillars of Wisdom Trust; Faber and Faber (Faber and Gwyer); Thomas Yoseloff (Golden Cockerel Press); The National Library of Wales (for the Gregynog Press); Jonathan Cape; Lettice Sandford (Golden Hours Press and Boar's Head Press); the Nonesuch Press; The Folio Society; and Lewis Allen (Allen Press). Where we have been unable to contact other publishers we hope that they will excuse the inclusion of illustrations from their books without acknowledgement.

1

EARLY YEARS

1902–1925

Blair Rowlands Hughes-Stanton was born in London on 22 February 1902. The second of four children, he was the only son of Sir Herbert Hughes-Stanton (né Herbert Hughes), the highly respected landscape painter and President of the Royal Society of Painters in Water-colours. Herbert's brother, Talbot Hughes, was a painter of decorative pictures and portraits, and their father, William Hughes, was also a painter — of flowers and still life. Herbert added Stanton, another family name, to his surname because at one point the three Hughes painters were exhibiting simultaneously at the Academy, and because the two brothers also shared a studio with the consequent confusion of their post.

Herbert Hughes-Stanton (1870–1937) was a very self-disciplined artist but patently enjoyed his work, being confident in his aims and abilities. By the end of the First World War, during which he had been an accredited War Artist, he was firmly established as one of the leading contemporary landscape painters. Rodney Thomas, a great friend of Blair's, remembered being told by Herbert, 'a lovely, gentle man', how he had decided to become a painter, quite accidently. 'He used to paint for fun and one day he was walking along looking in a few shop windows and there was a painting by Herbert Hughes — himself! He saw it on sale in the window for £60. "£60! In that case I'll go on painting!"'[1]

By the age of 16, Herbert had already exhibited his first painting. Although his tenor voice was good enough for him to have considered a singing career, the momentum his painting had already built up was irresistible. He was self-taught, secretly borrowing paints and brushes from his father's studio. Landscape was always his passion: having absorbed the influences of Constable, Turner, Claude and the Impressionists he developed a style of his own independent of any school, clique or ism. He was making his own living by the age of 20, but had to wait for several years and establish himself properly before he could marry his beloved 'Bessie', Elizabeth Cobden Rowlands, granddaughter of Richard Cobden, and daughter of William Rowlands of court jewellers Rowlands and Frazer.

Bessie, Blair's mother, a gentle and sensible woman, was a source of comfort and strength to 'Bertie', but she was also ambitious for him.[2] She cannot have been disappointed. He was awarded Gold Medals at the Paris Salon in the first years of the century and paintings were bought by the

French Government for the Luxembourg Museum. Official recognition in Britain came slightly later, beginning with the Tate's purchase of a painting in 1908, and culminating in the presidency of the RSPWC (1920), the status of Royal Academician (1921), and his knighthood (1923). Gratifying as such honours must have been, Herbert was happiest painting quietly in France, Hampshire, Suffolk and the wilder parts of Britain.

A traveller and collector, Herbert became an authority on furniture, painting and architecture. The houses in Kensington,[3] Titchfield in Hampshire and later Haut de Cagnes in the South of France were filled with beautiful and extraordinary things. His daughters would tell of the embarrassment of being picked up from school by a car sprouting with halberds and other paraphernalia.[4] His brother Talbot, a frail but jolly man (who lived with his red-haired model, Alice), restored the portraits that Herbert collected and was also responsible for some of the figures in Herbert's landscapes. Pneumonia contracted in Japan in 1925 left Herbert with a weak chest which necessitated spending the winters in France but did not prevent him from working prolifically until his death in 1937.

Blair Hughes-Stanton's life was to be as productive as his father's, but by no means as tranquil. His early education took place at Colet Court, the preparatory school for St Paul's, where he does not seem to have distinguished himself except for winning a prize for a free-hand drawing of Corinthian columns with perfectly straight lines. He was appalled at the prospect of attending St Paul's as a day-boy and staying at home with his three sisters. He had developed a dislike for his 'overwhelming' older sister Beryl ('Barrel') ever since, years earlier, she had told their mother of what to him had been an idyllic and magical game of fairies in the garden with his two younger sisters, Chloris and Barbara, all three clothed in nothing but pale blue satin sashes. On the other hand he could think of no reasonable excuse, other than cost, for not being sent to boarding school. At the age of thirteen he took what he later regarded as one of the most important decisions of his life: he left home to join the Cadet School Ship HMS Conway. The First World War apparently legitimised his declared wish to be a sailor.

The three years on the training ship, with mathematics and navigation virtually the only subjects, did little for his formal education — his spelling remained eccentric and his punctuation virtually non-existent for the rest of his life — but provided the crucial escape from convention and contributed to the development of his innate perfectionist practicality. He emerged as a Senior Cadet Captain with an extra certificate which recorded his conduct and ability as 'V.G.' and would have allowed him to take his examination as Second Mate in the Merchant Marine after being three instead of four years at sea.

After the War, having failed the examinations to get into the Royal Navy, Blair was discussing his future one day with his father, who suddenly suggested that he might become an artist. Blair replied that it had

William Hughes   Elizabeth Rowlands

Below: Sir Herbert Hughes-Stanton

never occurred to him, but he was immediately won over by the observation that he would always be his own boss. He was given a piece of charcoal and was set to draw a wooden figure of a nun — for six months. He stayed in his father's studio for over a year developing the skills and absorbing the discipline required to make a living as an artist.

His formal training started in 1919 at the Byam Shaw School of Art. There the students were set to draw the figure of a laughing fawn for a

Blair Hughes-Stanton as a boy

whole year with a 6H pencil. According to Rodney Thomas, a student contemporary who became a lifelong friend, they were not allowed into the life room until they had done enough drawing of plaster casts. 'Nobody taught you anything at Byam Shaw. They were just in and out, in and out. Then they asked you to get out of the way and they'd draw it themselves quite nicely.'[5] An exception to this form of teaching was A. S. Hartrick, whom Blair admired as an artist but who 'could not cope with the antique figures'. He had known Gaugin and Van Gogh and was a friend of various artists in Paris but he was not allowed to talk about French art at the school. Then the sculptor Leon Underwood arrived to teach drawing. His influence on Blair and several of his contemporaries was to be considerable.

What Underwood taught was not how to draw, but what drawing was. In an interview with the author taped in 1979 BHS described in detail what this meant:

'Leon's teaching of drawing was a logical approach, not hand-and-eye, that sort of thing. He didn't encourage you to draw in line straight away.

Cadet Captain Blair Hughes-Stanton, 1918

You couldn't, and anyway the whole point of a good line drawing is what the line is expressing. If you've got a hard edge you can move your head around that and it will be the same, but if you've got an edge of something going slowly round it will alter all the time. In a good drawing you have an emphasis. In a Michelangelo for example, it isn't that he's just drawing thick and thin like this. He's drawing thick and thin because one part is uncertain and the other part is the edge. So what you are doing is making a statement. One can almost draw in contour but that's the very, very end. You can learn a formula. Leon didn't start with any contour at all. If you had to draw a bottom, you start to make a model of a sphere, push the sphere about, then you come to your contour in the end. You've been going round it all the time, so you know that at that point you can cut the edge off.' Rodney Thomas agrees that Underwood's theory of drawing was based on solid geometry paying attention to tones and shadows but ignoring colour. He remembers that Underwood could draw even if the light was coming from the wrong direction — by logic.[6]

In 1921 BHS was among the first students at the Leon Underwood School of Painting and Sculpture, Girdlers Road, Brook Green, Hammersmith. He initially attended only the evening life class. From 1922 he was officially attending the Royal Academy Schools, but he was to spend increasing amounts of time at Underwood's school, drawing from life all day. Fellow evening students included Henry Moore, Vivian Pitchforth, Rodney Thomas, Raymond Coxon and his wife Edna Ginessi ('Gin'). Among the full-time students were Gertrude Hermes, whom BHS was soon to marry, Mary Groom, Barbara Weekley, Nora Unwin, Eileen Agar, Velona Pilcher and Marion Mitchell.

It was the American Marion Mitchell (not Mary Groom as stated by Balston) who started the students wood-engraving. She had met and been encouraged by Robert Gibbings and had gone to Paris to study under Demetrius Galanis, the engraver most noted for his use of the multiple tool. She returned with a set of engraving tools, including one of these. The others bought boxwood blocks at T. N. Lawrence's and, sharing the tools, simply started drawing on the block in white line. They had to work out the techniques of wood-engraving for themselves as they knew no formulae or short-cuts, but learned quickly in the atmosphere of friendly competition. BHS was fascinated by the way that the white line altered his attitude to drawing. From the beginning he was less interested in contrasts between areas of black and white than in the tones that could be achieved by the close cutting of fine white lines, and very soon rejected the multiple tool to rely on his own eyesight and control.

As the students did not have a printing press they found a friendly printer who helped them because he 'liked Art'. Sometimes they made hand-prints. BHS's earliest surviving engravings ('The Song', 'The Hero', 'Bathers' and 'Problem M', all 1924) were printed by hand on Japanese tissue. This involved placing the paper over the inked block and rubbing the back with a metal burnisher, a spoon or the 'handle of a toothbrush with the pointed end filed down'. Once the paper was sticking all over, it was possible to work further on the black areas where more solidity was required. In fact, BHS thought that it was possible to print more sensitively by hand than with a press. On the other hand, he said that there was no need for such 'printing about once you got the cutting right', a reasonable sounding assertion, though even at the height of his powers as a wood-engraver there were always problems with the printing because of the extreme fineness of his lines.

Although his was a school mainly for drawing, painting and sculpture, Leon Underwood encouraged and joined his students in their new activity.

166

He approved of the discipline of printmaking.[7] His woodcuts probably inspired and influenced them technically and emotionally. Uninfluenced by what they saw as the more illustrative tradition of wood-engraving that was being taught at the Central School of Art (by Noel Rooke), the Royal College and other schools, the work of the Underwood group could develop in its own distinct direction. Wood-engraving for them was no longer merely a craft, a form of interpreting pen and ink drawing or the exact rendering of natural objects (usually connected with illustration and letter-press), but became a means of individual creative expression. The meaning of the image was more important than the form.

Blair Hughes-Stanton, c. 1926

In 1925 the incompatibility of these two schools of thought led Edward Gordon Craig, Ethelbert White, John Greenwood, Leon Underwood and his students, including BHS, to break away from the Society of Wood Engravers, founded five years earlier, to form the English Wood Engraving Society. Exhibitions were held annually in London at the St George's Gallery, in George Street, Hanover Square. This group concentrated initially on independent engravings, some in colour, for walls rather than books. They were popular and sold well. Commissions for book illustrations followed, and as these increased, the distinctions between the two groups became less clear and they re-amalgamated in 1932.[8] The Underwood group had by then set up its own magazine, The Island (1931), to express its belief in the supremacy of imagination and the 'realisation of the artistic self' over 'technical efficiency'. The four issues of the magazine contained contributions by Henry Moore, John Gould Fletcher, Lawrence Bradshaw, Ralph Chubb, Eileen Agar, Velona Pilcher and others, and included two of BHS's independent engravings, 'Vortex' and 'Nude' (both 1929).

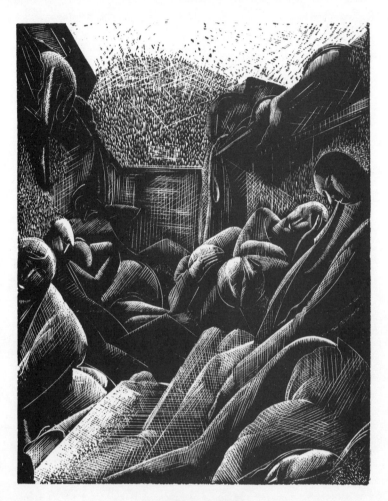

'3me Classe', 1925

Underwood's enthusiasms and influence were not limited to the studio. In 1923 he took BHS and Rodney Thomas to Iceland on a working holiday, here described by Christopher Neve:

'They landed at Reykjavik and made their way north to Husavik, hiring pack horses for the final stage of the journey and adding an edge of excitement by using only a primitive compass for navigation, perhaps as a gesture in the general direction of the simple life they had come to find. They were lent the school at Husavik and used it as a studio, it being the time of year when all pupils were required out in the fields to make hay during the short summer.'[9] Rodney Thomas remembers the competition in efficiency and self-sufficiency between the other two men: 'Blair was very organised — and Leon had been in the Artillery or something during the War and they both knew what they were doing. I was so very vague about everything. They had everything organised — do this and do that. I enjoyed myself, got on very well and all that ... but I got fed up with it after a time and I came back by myself.' He remembers a particularly vigorous argument at a road junction where BHS insisted that they go to the right and Underwood was adamant that it was only possible to go left. Feeling rather guilty about leaving his obstinate friend, Thomas went with the more experienced Underwood. After miles of tortuous tramping round a mountain they eventually came upon BHS sitting smugly at a cross roads.[10]

Subsequent working trips abroad were to be equally formative. In 1924 BHS went to Paris with Rodney Thomas, Henry Moore and others (including girls who shocked the French by not wearing stockings).[11] They sometimes went to the Académie St Julien. 'You went in and sat in some kind of arena. All these French sat drawing the model on the stage thing in the middle. It was the first time we'd had short poses. You would start with a long pose and then get shorter and shorter and shorter till it was a half-minute pose. In England when they taught drawing you'd have a model sitting there for a week in the same position. To have short poses with the model suddenly changing was lovely.'[12]

The stylistic influence of the Impressionists, especially Cézanne, and the Cubists, especially Picasso, can be seen in BHS's early paintings. These already show the beginnings of a lasting preoccupation with human figures, especially lovers, the result of years of drawing the figure from life. On the other hand, the strange symbolism and distortion of the tribal art in the Musée de l'Homme struck perhaps a deeper chord. This interest in ethnic art was shared with, indeed probably initiated by Underwood, who also transmitted his interest in palaeolithic art. Tribal art had, of course, had the same liberating impact on other artists, including Picasso and Braque. The young men also visited small galleries and had contacts in the Russian ballet.

In the summer of 1925 a large group from the school went to the Paris Exhibition, then on to Venice, Split in Yugoslavia, and, after a bout of food poisoning, back to Italy. In the course of this summer BHS saved Mary 'Lizzie' Groom from drowning and fell in love with Gertrude Hermes.

In December 1925 Leon Underwood left for a three year trip to the United States, leaving BHS in charge of the Brook Green school for a few months in case he should decide on an early return. By now BHS had left home and was sleeping on a camp bed at the house in Hammersmith of the artist John Cosmo Clark, who also allowed him to use his studio. Through Clark he met Eric Kennington, another resident of Hammersmith, and through him T. E. Lawrence, who was working on the manuscript and the production of *Seven Pillars of Wisdom*. This introduction led to the first of many commissions for engravings for books.

2

FIRST BOOKS

1926–1930

Blair Hughes-Stanton contributed 10 tail-piece engravings to T. E. Lawrence's *Seven Pillars of Wisdom* (1926). This extraordinary work included more than a hundred other wood-engravings and reproductions of photographs, pastels, watercolours and drawings by eminent contemporary artists including Clark and Kennington (who also designed the end-papers), William Roberts, Augustus John, Henry Lamb, Paul Nash, R. M. Young, Colin Gill, John S. Sargeant, William Rothenstein, and Frank Dobson. There was also one engraving by Gertrude Hermes.

83–5

A few copies, possibly as few as four, contained a further engraving by BHS illustrating the dedicatory poem to the mysterious 'S.A.', presumed to be Lawrence's friend Dahoum although Lawrence deliberately obscured the matter.[1] Exactly how many copies contained this extra engraving is not known as Lawrence seems to have been determined to keep this privately printed edition more literally private than most other so-called private press books. Copies were bound in different colours or styles. Some copies in unbound sheets were given to friends who then had them bound to their own requirements. Incomplete books, with fewer plates, were half-bound in leather and given to those who fought with him in Arabia; others were given to those involved in the production of the book; the remainder were sold to subscribers for thirty guineas, although their cost had already trebled that. Profit was not the object of the exercise.[2]

Lawrence's long-held interest in the private press tradition was given expression in this uniquely personal extravaganza. He closely supervised the entire production himself.[3] An indication of the intensity of his involvement is his request to BHS to ensure that the engravings had 'the balance of print about one black to eight white in area'.[4] 'Lawrence was impressed with the result: "Blair H–S is very subtle. People will go around goggling to know who it is."'[5] He did not, however, really understand the engravings and thought they were 'mad' — like the war itself.[6] He also commissioned BHS to design an X and a Z to complete a set of initial letters, originally designed by Edward Wadsworth for John Rodker of the Ovid Press, to be used as paragraph headings in the three line size and as chapter openings in a larger size. Lawrence went so far as to misspell a name in order to incorporate the X. The designs appear to be based on wood-engravings.[7]

The text and decorations were printed by Manning Pike, a trainee printer, with the assistance of H. J. Hodgson, a skilled pressman, who was later to work with BHS at the Gregynog Press. 'That's where I'd met him (Hodgson) you see. He'd been printing paper bags or something before and Manning Pike, who printed the book, had never printed before in his life. The two of them used to fight like cats and dogs, using up tons of hand-made paper, but they made a marvellous job at the end of it.'[8] That was one of BHS's more benign comments on the project. He did not like T. E. Lawrence: Rodney Thomas says BHS found him 'an aggressive little chap' and 'edgy'.[9] He must have felt an unease with the book which can be detected in his engravings. By 18 June 1926 he had already sold his copy for 100 guineas and, with a precipitancy that deeply shocked his more restrained parents, had married Gertrude on the proceeds.

Gertrude Hermes, *c.* 1926

Gertrude Anna Bertha Hermes, (1901–83), was born in Kent of German parents. Her father, Louis Augustus Hermes, was a designer and manufacturer of silk ties. After an early education in private schools she had attended Beckenham School of Art. In 1920 she went to Munich to stay with her aunt, the painter, Mary Hermes, who encouraged her to stay in Germany. She insisted on returning to England and attended the Leon Underwood School of Painting and Sculpture. There, as well as drawing, she took up the wood-engraving and sculpture for which she would be so well known. Before she married BHS in 1926 she had qualified for the finals of the Prix de Rome for engraving.[10] However, the birth of two children in quick succession (Judith, born 30 April 1927 and Simon, born 8 September 1928) restricted her time and capacity for work for the next few years.[11]

BHS with Judith and Simon, 1929/1930

86 BHS worked on miscellaneous projects during the mid-twenties, while continuing to paint in oils. He painted murals in Paris[12] and London.[13] He also made cover and title engravings for pamphlets of the poems *Alone* (1927) and *Self to Self* (1928) by Walter de la Mare, published by Faber and Gwyer. In addition, his involvement with the Gate Theatre, which was under the arches at Charing Cross Station, and with its American instigator, Velona Pilcher, another of Underwood's students, resulted in a variety of work. As well as scene painting, BHS engraved seven of the playbills for the first season (1927–28). A note on the last of these reads: 'The Gate Theatre Press invites playgoers to observe that these playbills they are reading are held in increasing esteem by people interested in hand printing, acquainted with the best of the Old English playbills preserved in the Enthoven Collection at the South Kensington Museum, and appreciative of modern wood-engravings. Sets for the Season 1927–28 are being collected by connoisseurs. A few of these sets — or single bills to complete

broken sets — may still be bought at one shilling each sheet. There are nine of these playbills altogether. Seven have wood engravings, especially designed for each play, by Blair H–S.; and two — the first two in the seven — are particularly acceptable, having been printed by the Golden Cockerel Press.' The note is signed 'V.P.'

During the same period BHS made engravings to head four articles by Velona Pilcher for the American publication *Theatre Arts Monthly* (1926– 27), and illustrated the reading version of her play *The Searcher, A War Play* (1929). Although this was not published until January 1929 the engravings were done in the rougher and less controlled, spiky style of two years earlier.

On this book a cryptic lecture note of Blair's reports a 'disagreement over typography'. Although no details are recorded, one might presume that he was less than happy with the text, with the extensive stage directions in black and the dialogue in red, indented and often capriciously stepped or otherwise arranged. The front flap of the dust cover reads: '. . . Miss Pilcher is the first English writer to correlate experiments in the art of the theatre into a poetic form, and this purpose has come somewhat of a challenge to current dramatic criticism.' There then follow five snippets of uniformly hostile criticism.

Different in almost every way was the work, in collaboration with Gertrude, on Bunyan's *The Pilgrim's Progress* (1928). This impressive folio edition, bound in black vellum, and with ten specials printed on vellum, was published by the Cresset Press, but printed and made at the Shakespeare Head Press, Stratford on Avon, by Bernard Newdigate, whose experience and perfectionism in orthodox typography and printing were beyond dispute and compare. It was perhaps the first real test of the two young artists' ability to harness their rampant expressionism and fit it into the restricting reins of a letterpress production. There were problems. Newdigate apparently disapproved of the engravings and thought that they should be in black line, like Eric Gill's. BHS told him that he was not interested in doing things like Eric Gill.[14] There were, as was to be usual, problems with the printing, as BHS told Paul Collet: 'They did a number of copies on vellum and the proofs arrived at the Cresset Press and they all looked like patent-leather boots, completely filled in. Dennis Cohen said we must go down there and see what can be done about it. I'd never touched a printing press in my life, you see, and I only had sort of, working with Manning Pike on *Seven Pillars*. I went down there and they were printing on a big handpress and I had a terrific morning. The machine-man seemed quite a nice chap to me and it took a long time to get him round with "Wouldn't it be a conquest if we could do it" . . . and we managed it. Then he said, "Well all the vellum's a different thickness," all that sort of thing. They were always worrying about pressure and make-ready. I don't think it's necessary at all.'[15]

The following year BHS and Gertrude contributed an engraving each to another Cresset Press production, *The Apocrypha* (1929), printed this time

87
87

88–9

90

14   'Turkish Bath', 1929 (reduced from 7 × 9 in) ◀

by the Curwen Press. The twelve other artists were Leon Underwood, Stephen Gooden, René Ben Sussan, Mary Groom, Eric Jones, Wladislaw Skoczylas, Hester Sainsbury, Frank Medworth, Eric Kennington, Eric Ravilious, John Nash and D. Galanis (of multiple tool fame). BHS's engraving of 'Susannah and the Elders' shows the central figure in black, described with very few white engraved lines, surrounded by a contrasting white area and with all the detail reserved for the subordinate background.   90

His other engravings of this period show similar arrangements and techniques. Most notable among these is the startling engraving entitled 'Emancipation of Woman'. Many have wondered about the significance of   171 this powerful 'personal' engraving with its two terrified males looking on in flaccid horror at the resplendent female in the centre of the image. Could it not have been inspired by Susannah's triumph over the Elders? Another engraving of the same year, 'The Turkish Bath', re-uses the features of the   14 stepped pool and the vaulted, columned interior. It is clearly a fantasy and interesting to compare with his wife's earlier and grotesquely more realistic version, engraved in 1926. On the other hand a certain amount of personal   16 significance in the 'Emancipation of Woman' print should not be ruled out given the confusion and disturbance shown in 'Vortex' and 'Maze' at this   170 the beginning of a turbulent but very productive period.

His links with private presses now established, it was in fact his involvement with the Gate Theatre which led to his first association with the Golden Cockerel Press, then under the auspices of Robert and Moira Gibbings. *Maya* (1930), a play by Simon Gantillon, paraphrased into now   94–5 painfully dated English by Virginia and Frank Vernon, had been one of the first plays performed at the Gate. BHS had done an engraving for the playbill which had pleased the playwright. When Gibbings asked to publish the play Gantillon suggested that BHS should illustrate it. *Maya* concerns the life of a prostitute, 'a moth or butterfly whose wings are painted by every man in the colours of his desire', a topic which gave full scope to BHS's interest in the human figure and male/female relations.

There were the inevitable rows over printing the dark blocks with their increasingly confident and increasingly fine white lines. 'Mr Gibbings was not very good at printing my rather black wood-engravings. He used a lot of ink. We ended hardly on speaking terms. The paper was practically impossible. Also, they couldn't have damped it much because I've printed on paper as rough as that. And of course nobody in those days seemed to think of letting inks down a slight amount but you still got your coverage. Of course it might have been all right for the type, but even then I think it used to start getting round the type and accumulating so that they were always having to scrub out.'[16]

In 1934 John Gould Fletcher opined fulsomely on the subject of the *Maya* engravings: 'These cuts are not so well known as they should be, owing to the fact that in the original edition they were printed on the wrong kind of paper, which led to an effect of baldness and hardness which was unfortunate and entirely alien to Hughes-Stanton's intention. One need

'Turkish Bath', by Gertrude Hermes, 1926 ◀

only take the remarkable frontispiece, or any of the delightful tail-pieces, to understand what the artist is henceforward driving at. Here, if anywhere, the modern woodcut breaks free of the last vestige of old pictorial tradition, and becomes a form in itself, an independent entity made up of areas of light and dark, an almost musical rearrangement of form, expressive if you will, of human sensuality but also of that universal human yearning of which sensuality is perhaps only the most convenient symbol to hand. The woodcut here becomes no longer a direct illustration, nor an ornament of the text (though its function as ornament is greater), but a sculptural summary of intention upon which the eye can rest in the intervals of reading, something akin to a musical accompaniment of the words. From the time of the "Maya" designs Hughes-Stanton was destined only to elaborate upon his own discovery, to bring it to the last pitch of perfection.'[17]

John Gould Fletcher had written a similarly appreciative article on BHS and Gertrude Hermes five years earlier, in 1929.[18] During the late twenties BHS had continued to paint energetically and was disappointed when Arthur Tooth, of the Tooth Gallery, failed to make him a house artist after initial encouraging overtures. The slump had seriously affected the art market and commissions were few. Times were hard for the couple with their two young babies. The last straw was the 1928 flood of the Thames, when all their engravings and blocks were soaked as their basement flat in Hammersmith Terrace was inundated. With the idea that it would be cheaper to live in the country they moved to Hacheston in Suffolk. The plan was to continue painting and then sell the work in London.

The move, however proved disastrous for the marriage. Gertrude was used to the vibrant society of their Hammersmith neighbours, who included Dick and Naomi Mitchison and Alan and Gwen Herbert, and was shocked at the isolation of the country, compounded as it was by Blair's discovery of the cheery calm and beery balm of the village pub. He enjoyed listening to the talk of the country working men and the easy male matiness after his solitary day painting or working on the house (the first of several conversions of delapidated buildings). He felt completely at ease amongst them, while his charm and humour led to their ready acceptance of him. This love of association with working men was no mere affectation but fulfilled some basic psychological need. It stayed with him for the rest of his life, much to the chagrin of his successive wives, each one deserted nightly. The root of it may possibly be traced to the strong influence of D. H. Lawrence with whom BHS was working on the folio volume of poetry, *Birds, Beasts and Flowers*, published in 1930, just after Lawrence's 91–3 death.

They had met through Frieda Lawrence's daughter, Barbara (Barby) Weekley Barr, who had also attended the Leon Underwood School. The two men appear to have been similar in temperament, charming but irascible, and to have got on well together. In a letter from his Villa Mirenda in Florence, dated 26 May 1928, Lawrence had written to BHS:

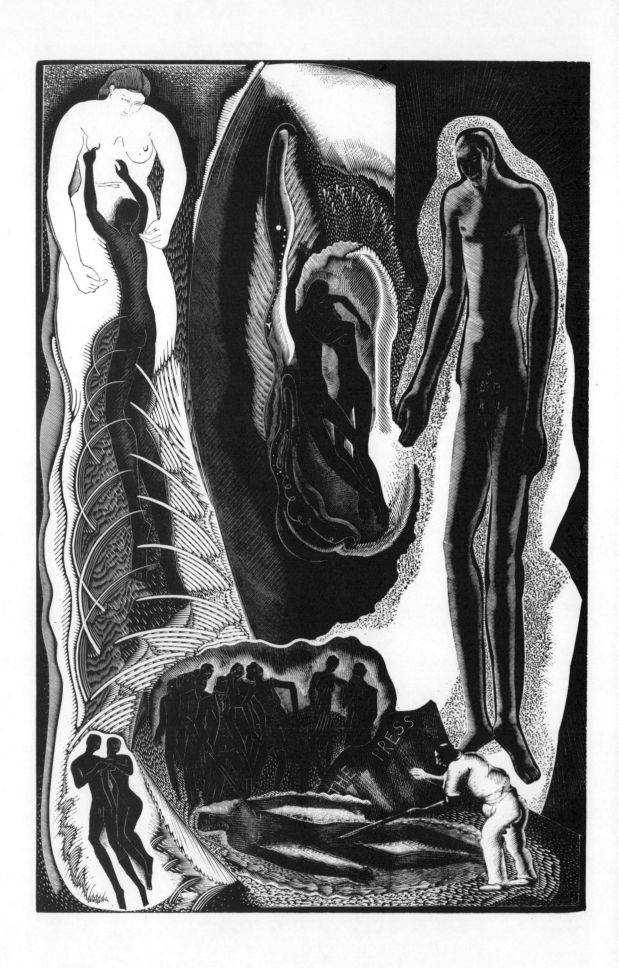

18   'A Man Died', 1930 (reduced from 12 × 8 in)

Dear Blair,

Nice of you to order my novel [*Lady Chatterley's Lover*]. I'm getting to the last proofs now, & the printer is printing fast. So I hope soon we can send you your copy. And I hope you'll think it worth it.

So there is to be another bambino, to go with Judith: not a Holofernes, I hope. It's a bit of a handful for you. But after all, I think perhaps the material responsibility of children saves one from a lot of useless worry about the world, the soul and the devil. I think children must make life warmer to one, so you're really the winner. Perhaps if I'd have had children I'd have been a comfortable body with all my novels circulating like steam among all the safe people, & everybody pleased.

I expect we shall come to England in August, then surely we shall see you, as we think to stay six weeks or so. I remember so well the beer & skittles in your basement (forgive the word, but it *is* too low down). And if ever you all feel like coming & camping in this house, Judith & Holofernes and all, then here it'll be.

Many good wishes from us both.

D. H. Lawrence.[19]

Working with Lawrence so shortly after the furore which followed the publication of *Lady Chatterley's Lover* in 1928 and the seizure of paintings from Lawrence's exhibition the following year, BHS cannot but have been excited and inspired by the liberating philosophy of the older man. Lawrence in turn seems to have taken an encouraging interest in BHS's work. In a letter from Germany, dated 30 August 1929, he wrote in response to BHS's news of the flood, his financial difficulties, and request to illustrate *Birds, Beasts and Flowers*:

Dear Blair,

Your letter reached me only today. So sorry about the house & cash. Perhaps you aren't quite bold enough, in your work: one has to be either downright take-it-or-leave-it, or else one has to love 'em and give 'em what they want. So damned difficult anyhow.

But I am very pleased for you to make drawings for *Birds Beasts*. Don't know anything about the Cresset Press — but if they are going ahead, tell them *not* to approach Secker direct, but to write to L. E. Pollinger. Curtis Brown Ltd. 6 Henrietta St. W.C.2 and get him to arrange it. He will fix better terms all round, for me & you as well. Tell me the scheme — how many copies, at what price, how many signed — and tell them, if they like I'll do them a new foreword, on the essential nature of poetry or something like that. Tell them that if they print in front: These poems are printed from the Collected Poems of D.H.L., published by Martin Secker — or something to that effect, that goes a long way with Martin Secker: but not to say it if it harms the new edition — yours.

Yes, you must work for the limited-edition people now — it's the only way to make money. And I must keep my eye open for any book that you might do. Perhaps later on, another unexpurgated *Pansies* — that sells.

Well, I'm glad you like your children, for most modern parents emphatically don't, no matter how much they wash and comb 'em.

We are here for about two more weeks — then presumably Italy. Frieda limps with her foot — I cough — the scenery is very nice.

Which of my pictures don't you like, & why?

Regards to you both and for god's sake, don't go into a *cellar*. If it must be among the corpses, let it at least be a modest above ground mausoleum!

D. H. Lawrence[20]

BHS was permanently affected by Lawrence's belief in the vital importance and indeed rightness of responding to one's basic animal instincts

20   'Rebirth', 1930 (reduced from 12 × 8 in)

rather than to any superficial, taught morality, and by his new and frighteningly frank, if ultimately unresolved, examination of relations between the sexes. The poems in *Birds, Beasts and Flowers* attempt to show the relationship between the poet and the object of his poetry, the suffusion of the one by the other, a physical rather than an intellectual process. BHS was interested in and disturbed by the same questions of love and sensuality and his approach to his work was always unashamedly 'personal' rather than attempting to be completely objective. As a result the engravings carry a high emotional charge. Here at last was a collaboration about which BHS never expressed any doubts or quibbles.

The Hughes-Stantons visited Lawrence in France a month before he died, as related by Barby:

> In early February, Lawrence had left Bandol for the Ad Astra sanatorium at Vence in the Maritime Alps. Frieda went with him; I stayed on at the Villa Beau Soleil.
> A friend of mine met them at Nice, and motored them to the Sanatorium.
> 'Blair has been as kind as an angel to me,' wrote Lawrence from there, adding, 'Here is £10 for housekeeping.' To this Frieda put a post-script. 'Be careful with the money.' This admonition impressed me so much, that when Blair and his wife came to see me. I gave them only a few rags of boiled meat from the soup for lunch, and offended them.[21]

The depth of BHS's regard for Lawrence and grief at his death can be seen in the large block engraved in 1930 entitled 'A Man Died'. It shows Lawrence towering above his own dead body which is being castrated by 'The Press' and stabbed by chortling critics. A mother and child fill the top left-hand corner while two entwined couples look mournfully on.   18

A matching block of the same year, 'Rebirth', celebrates the beginning   20
of BHS's affair with Ida Graves, poetess, reader for the Stage Society and (later) novelist.[22] Although it would be unfair to blame D. H. Lawrence personally for the failure of the Hughes-Stantons' marriage, the connection between these two blocks is an indication of his influence over BHS's thinking at that time. DHL had warned Gertrude to expect trouble with Blair, but she must already have been aware that even without their difficult circumstances they could not be happy together. BHS was unready for the responsibility of parenthood. In addition, although outwardly an ideal couple of fellow artists, whose deep spiritual friendship would indeed endure throughout their lives, they were incompatible sexually. BHS felt somehow 'embarrassed' with her from the first day of their marriage.[23] Ida, by contrast, offered him 'Lawrentian sex'.[24] For the next three years the affair was to cloud not only his family life but also his professional relationships at the renowned Gregynog Press, owned as it was by Calvinistic Methodists, who naturally did not approve of such behaviour. On the other hand the relationship energised an output of inspired work for Gregynog, and later his own and other presses, which lasted until the outbreak of the Second World War, nine years later, and which was to prove the best of his career.

c

3

THE GREGYNOG PRESS

1930–1933

Gregynog Hall in the hills of Montgomeryshire (as readers may be aware thanks to Dorothy Harrop's excellent and exhaustive study *The Gregynog Press*, Private Libraries Association, 1980), is a large house with extensive stables and other outhouses set in a landscaped estate. It was owned in the thirties by the Davies sisters, Gwendoline and Margaret (Gwen and Daisy), and housed their great collection of paintings, which was later bequeathed to the National Museum of Wales. Their original intention had been to create a cultural centre of Welsh arts and crafts for the Welsh people. However, enthusiasm for these crafts waned and apart from regular musical events the Press became the sole embodiment of their wish, with its products paradoxically prized all over the world.

Crucial to the whole enterprise was Dr Thomas Jones ('T.J.'), Assistant and later Deputy Secretary to the Cabinet. The sisters relied totally on him for all advice and decisions. Robert Maynard, as artist controller, had been responsible for the day to day running of the press since its establishment in 1922 and had been joined by his friend Horace Bray in 1924. They shared the responsibility for the illustrations and for the overall artistic and typographical quality of the productions. After nine and seven years respectively, during which time the reputation of the press had been firmly established, the two artists resigned to set up the Raven Press. The isolation of Gregynog, the apparent lack of appreciation of their efforts by the owners, and increasing friction and misunderstandings with the Press Board all contributed to their disenchantment and led to their departure in the late summer of 1930.

Hugh Blaker, artist and connoisseur, who had earlier recommended Maynard to the Davies, now suggested as their replacement the Hughes-Stantons, who, although young, already enjoyed a reputation for their wood-engravings and sculpture. As well as the works to which both had contributed (*Seven Pillars of Wisdom*, *Pilgrim's Progress*, and the *The Apocrypha*), Gertrude had also illustrated *A Florilege* (1930) for the Swan Press. Blaker recommended BHS for his modernism which he considered would keep the press in the van of book production.[1] The sisters were not immediately convinced. Harrop quotes the shocked reaction, recorded in a letter to T.J., of the Calvinist Gwen Davies to 'Susannah and the Elders', BHS's engraving in the Cresset Press's *Apocrypha*: 'Oh dear! Do you think we can ever woo him from these delectable ladies? They will never do for Gregynog! That will have to be made perfectly clear.'[2]

90

After a vetting by T.J., the Hughes-Stantons were invited to Gregynog for the week-end, 9–12 May 1930, during which BHS suggested that instead of employing him and Gertrude as controller and artist respectively, the owners should invite William McCance, a Scottish painter, sculptor and art critic for *The Spectator*, to be controller, with himself as artist, as he had no wish to deal with administration and wished only to 'cut wood'.[3] As McCance was married to the wood-engraver Agnes Miller-Parker, the two wives were to be employed as wood-engravers on an annual advance retainer of £100. The McCances impressed Gwen Davies and T.J. and the quartet was duly appointed.

Gertrude had not in fact wanted to go to Wales but Blair's appointment would almost certainly have been in jeopardy had she refused. The small size of her retainer left her morally free to continue with her sculpture which was, however, difficult to transport and sell from the isolation of mid-Wales. The fact that BHS made frequent and extended trips to London, 'to keep in touch', exacerbated her misery.[4]

The two men, like their predecessors, had no experience of typography or printing when they arrived. So, with the reputation of the Press at stake, the Press Board decided to send them off to commercial printing firms for a short period of intensive training. BHS's month at the Baynard Press was of little benefit, spent as it was largely in the composing room.[5] The new recruits were lucky, however, in that the Press had a skilled compositor and printer in Herbert Hodgson, skilled pressmen such as Idris Jones and a binder of great calibre, George Fisher. Dora Herbert-Jones, the Secretary to the Press, was also concerned with the maintenance of high typographical standards. She, poor woman, had the invidious position of go-between between the Press and the Board and it was she who invariably took the brunt of the anger and frustrations of the artists.

They were frustrated at having to complete *The Plays of Euripides* (1931) before being able to go on with their own work. By the end of October BHS had already displayed his 'violent temper'.[6] He and Idris Jones had repaired the Albion handpress, as the *Euripides* was occupying the main press. By December both BHS and McCance had done weeks of work on *The Lovers' Song Book*, by W. H. Davies, only to have their typography and engravings condemned. BHS wrote to Miss Davies in 1961:

t-p, 96–7

'I am afraid I rather played around with the indentation of the poems, but they were so light and easy to read it did not seem to matter as they looked so much better on the page (W. H. Davies also did not object). I also did small engraved initial letters, rather unorthodox and little tail pieces to fill up the page. But apparently it was all wrong typographically according to some old typographer [Stanley Morison, as BHS knew perfectly well], and so they decided not to publish, it was all printed except for the colophon so the whole edition was scrapped. I was allowed six copies including a vellum copy. I think six other copies were also partially bound. It was probably one of these you saw at the National Library. It was rather sad and I still think it was a nice little book and not as outragious [sic] as was made out. I nearly walked out, but settled down and did the *Comus*. This was also done on the hand press.'[7]

Above and opposite: Gregynog Christmas Card, 1930

An unillustrated version was later published by the Press, but although orthodox and correct is perhaps not as interesting as the banned original, which was regarded as too erotic for the conservative Gregynog clientele, as well as being a typographical nightmare. The comments of Stanley Morison on the subject are now well enough known.[8] Briefly, he expressed the opinion that although creative licence should be allowed, such self-

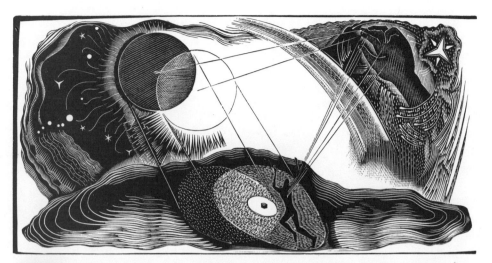

BENEATH the spaceless dome of the soul's firmament
he liveth in the glow of a celestial fire, $*$ $*$ $*$ $*$
fed by whose timeless beams our small obedient sun
is as a cast-off satellite, that borroweth $*$ $*$ $*$ $*$
from the great Mover of all; and in the light of light
man's little works, strewn on the sands of time, sparkle
like cut jewels in the beatitude of God's countenance.

The Testament of Beauty $*$ $*$ $*$ $*$ $*$ $*$ $*$ *Robert Bridges*

expression as was displayed in *The Lovers' Song Book* engravings, as well as
in the 'too apocryphallic' Christmas card (1930), was ill-suited to the
conservative craftsmanship of printing and should rather have its outlet in
other media.

McCance had written to ask Morison if he would come and hint to **BHS**
that the blocks were unsuitable:

One of my difficulties here is keeping a leash on Stanton — he just engraves quicker than one can breathe. We have now had a kind of clash with the directors over the book of poems of W. H. Davies. Stanton has produced some miniature caligraphic initial letters mixed up with figures which I personally don't care for very much, but the book has been mostly in his hands and he would like to stand by it. I have also to adopt a certain loyalty to him.[9]

McCance had had the same trouble restraining BHS on the Christmas card: 'Stanton has a perfect itch for engraving which amounts almost to a disease, started on one engraving and just continued while there was still time, and my problem of shaping it as it went on.'[10] Some of Morison's reply offended the Press Board but his typographical judgement that BHS's work was unsuitable was accepted as final.

Morison later wrote to McCance after a meeting with BHS: 'I have seen Mr Stanton and recognise him for a very energetic youngster likely to perturbate the Angles, as well as the Scots, and certainly the Welsh. I thought his engravings of the Comus lady a very fine piece.'[11] Praise indeed!

The Welsh were certainly perturbated, although Gwen Davies initially seems to have approved the engravings for the card, which lost the press many subscribers: 'I think they are very good and feel much relieved!'[12] Two months later, however, her concern to find suitable material for BHS to illustrate smacks of desperation: 'I saw Mr Blaker yesterday. He was strongly of the opinion that Hughes-Stanton should be given something quite prosaic to illustrate and that he should try his hand at portraits, landscapes, architecture etc. — anything to get him away from his elongated females!'[13] They did not succeed.

With *Euripides* still occupying the main press until mid-1931, BHS's next book also had to be printed by Idris Jones on the handpress. BHS collaborated in the design and the printing. Subtitled *A Maske presented at Ludlow Castle, 1634*, with Ludlow castle providing the rather tenuous Welsh connection, *Comus* (1931) is illustrated with a wood-engraved frontispiece and the five characters in costume. Two smaller images of Sabrina, clad in a skilfully engraved diaphanous garment, decorate the title and final pages. Except in the frontispiece where the Attendant Spirit is shown descending into the 'Wildewood', the tall elegant characters, so suited to the tall folio format, stand out on the blank Japanese vellum page. This feature of the cleared background is relatively unusual in BHS engravings. John Gould Fletcher remarked on these figures: 'He now began to use black and white with the fullest freedom and variation into a range of greys that continually suggests, if it does not state, colour; and he now also developed his somewhat flat and arbitrarily distorted drawing of the female form into a goddess shape that seems to have strayed out of the Italian Renaissance somewhere between Botticelli and Michelangelo, and to have wandered from there straight into our 20th century after a brief but important sojourn with William Blake. The "Comus" illustrations are delicious.'[14]

BHS also engraved the title. The letter forms he took from *The Moyllus Alphabet*, 'A Newly Discovered Treatise on Classic Letter Design, Printed

98–103

at Parma by Damianus Moyllus, circa 1480. Reproduced in facsimile with an introduction by Stanley Morison.' (Officina Bodoni, 1927.) BHS was obviously keen to avoid further typographical mistakes.

Letter C from *The Moyllus Alphabet*

Comus was the first book to have the binding designed by BHS. With help from the skilled George Fisher and after practising himself with the various finishing tools he produced for the special binding a reasonably restrained design of blind and gilt tooled lines, a contrast nevertheless with the yet more austere designs of his predecessors.[15] Harrop quotes Fisher's opinion of BHS's binding designs in general: 'They interested me more than they pleased me in that, while they afforded me ample opportunity to display my skill as a finisher, I considered them more suited to the decoration of the printed page than to a tooled leather cover.' Harrop counters these faintly damning remarks: 'Despite Fisher's reservations, the six Hughes-Stanton bindings remain for many collectors the most exciting and sought after of all the Gregynog bindings.'[16]

Harrop also records the artists' irritation at the amount of work required of them on ephemera which interrupted their weightier undertakings. Such work included two new press devices by BHS. The workload did not, however, preclude a visit to Paris in the summer of 1931.[17]

BHS's next book was *Caniadau* (1932), a volume of poetry in Welsh by 104–5 W. J. Gruffydd. It has been judged an undistinguished book typographically, a result of the controller's inexperience, but interesting none the less.[18] It was printed on grey hand-made paper which was not particularly suitable for the engravings. An overall depressing appearance was avoided by the use of Tyrian red for the headings, title, press device and shadow initials, all but the headings engraved by BHS and again adapted from the Moyllus Alphabet. The type chosen for the book was Eric Gill's Perpetua which had been recently issued by the Monotype Corporation. Delays in publication were caused by waiting for the italic version to be issued and it was finally decided to print the italic sections in roman in more of the red instead. The red of the paper covering the boards of the ordinary copies was achieved by using an inked roller. The effect with the grey spine and gilt titling is elegant and warm. BHS again designed the special binding of brown levant morocco with panels of vertical gilt lines.

Letters from BHS to McCance, who was away for Christmas 1931, detail their continuing feuds with the Board over such matters as the *Esope* colophon, of which the directors did not approve, and McCance's consultation with experts (such as Morison and Meynell) without their consent. BHS anticipated further squabbles after the printing staff refused to take orders from T.J. over the controller's head to reprint the colophon in his absence.[19]

By this time Gertrude's unhappiness and commitments to her children led to difficulty in honouring her obligations to the Press. She was supposed to be working on roughly thirty engravings for *The Natural History of Selborne* by Gilbert White. The Board was becoming increasingly impatient at her inability to produce, oblivious as they were as to the reasons. By March 1932 she had left Gregynog and moved to London, staying temporarily with Leon and Mary Underwood. She attempted to continue with the work on *Selborne* but her contract was terminated in June 1932 and the project shelved. The half-dozen completed engravings were finally published by the revived Gregynog Press, over fifty years later.[20]

Gertrude had earlier declined to illustrate Sir Robert Vansittart's *The Singing Caravan*, which was eventually designed and illustrated with only a frontispiece by McCance. Ladizesky records the unflattering verdict of T. E. Lawrence (who had recommended the book to the press) on what BHS would have made of it, indicating perhaps that the antipathy that BHS had felt towards him was mutual:

'A Hughes-Stanton version of Tauz the great camel would not have been to my taste. Some essential points of a camel thoroughbred would have been overlooked: and besides the light fantasy of the poems would not go with wood engravings . . . . I am glad you [McCance] are doing this book. H–S wrote to me that he did not like it: but then he is a person of unusual mind, who demands a great deal of his books. The Caravan was too thin for him. Probably he dislikes meringues and eclairs, trifles and omlettes souflées.'

This last assumption, at least, happened to be completely untrue. Later in the letter however he was less harsh: 'I've also ordered an Erewhon. That was a very good idea. A fair Erewhon is necessary. Now Erewhon would "carry" Hughes-Stanton.'[21]

110–13   That again is a debatable matter of opinion. *Erewhon*, by Samuel Butler, published in February 1933, is perhaps the book least suited to BHS's style. The 29 small engravings that served as chapter headings are obviously illustrations rather than his preferred personal interpretations. T.J. was concerned at the lack of consistency in the quality of the engravings as they appeared and asked McCance if he could subtly suggest that some of the less successful engravings be dropped so as not to detract from the better ones.[22] This may not have happened as there remain 29 engravings and the criticism of inconsistency is still valid when the set as a whole is examined. Newdigate's praise of the 'presswork of such uncanny perfection' is noted by Harrop[23] and her own typographical criticisms are illustrated in her book.[24] The 'very eccentric', 'peculiar', 'odd' design of the special binding[25] can perhaps be demystified by describing it as simply phallic — not an alien concept to a man in the throes of a torrid affair. Harrop writes that the binding 'in brown polished levant morocco . . . has been much admired, though possibly for the sheer virtuosity displayed in the tooling.'

In the course of 1932 BHS was asked by Christopher Sandford, who regarded him as the Prince of the new movement of engravers, and whose wife Lettice was one of many engravers greatly influenced by him, to make engravings for *The Tragicall History of Doctor Faustus* (1932).[26] This was   106–9 the first of nine volumes of Marlowe's works planned by Christopher Sandford and F. J. Newbery, and was printed for the Golden Hours Press at the Chiswick Press. David Chambers explains the genesis of the Golden Hours Press and the Boar's Head Press (whose *Primeval Gods* was to be illustrated by BHS in 1934): 'Though the Boar's Head was established in 1930 primarily as an outlet for Lettice and Christopher [Sandford]'s artistic and literary abilities, the Golden Hours Press was suggested to Newbery and the Romanes brothers as a means of getting work for the Chiswick Press when the depression made this hard to find . . .' Chambers goes on to record the foundering of this project: '. . . three quarto volumes were issued, quarter bound in red niger, with Cockerell marbled-cloth sides, *Faustus* illustrated by Blair Hughes-Stanton, *The Jew of Malta* by Eric Ravilious, and *Hero and Leander* by Lettice Sandford. The text for all nine volumes was set, and corrected by Sandford, but only about forty copies of the first three were sold, and Newbery had the rest of the type distributed without prior reference to him. Those that were issued are handsome volumes, with a fine series of engravings, and the texts three of the most important from Marlowe's work. There were to have been copies printed on vellum, but these were never done. The balance of the edition was taken over by Hollis & Carter, and issued in buckram boards, still pleasing volumes for all their remaindered state.'[27]

The two prospectuses issued for the *Faustus* included BHS engravings from the book. Chambers has remarked that these engravings are cut more openly for the surface of the rough English hand-made paper, than those to be printed on Japanese vellum, BHS's preferred surface. Sandford's insistence on the clarity of the fine white lines was rewarded by black but clean printing from the pressmen at Chiswick. Even so the perennial danger of overinking to retain the solidity of the blacks and thus of losing the finer white lines was something that BHS took further steps to avoid in *The Revelation of Saint John the Divine*, produced for the Gregynog Press in   114–21 the same year, 1932.

This book is regarded by many as his masterpiece. The incredible fineness of the white lines, almost impossible to reproduce, was only feasible thanks to the skilled presswork of Herbert Hodgson. A crucial factor, after the surface of the paper, the pressure of the press, and so on, was the consistency of the ink. Tins of ink still at Gregynog have BHS's writing on them: 'Special mixing to consistency of German Ink. BLUE-BLACK in Tone.' The ink was let down with copper-plate oil, resulting in a longer ink without too much loss of intensity in the black areas.

The text appears to serve merely as a vehicle to display the virtuosity of the engravings. There was, in fact, initially an economic reason for this apparent imbalance. The depression had necessitated a cutback in the publication of books, such as *Erewhon*, with a lot of text, which, being hand-set, were expensive to produce. McCance, reluctantly, was forced into the 'delicate arms' of the 'precious book'. It was cheaper to make thinner books with more pictures, making more use of the artists who had to be paid anyway.[28]

Revelation was presumably BHS's own choice. D. H. Lawrence had suggested some years before that he illustrate it and had wanted to discuss the symbolism with him. BHS had been thinking that perhaps the Cresset Press might have published it. The excitement that he felt at his involvement in the Gregynog production of this volume stayed with him for the rest of his life. He told Paul Collet: 'The compositor and I were simply working side by side. I'd never had an opportunity like that before to really go chapter by chapter and work out how far it was going to go. I cut the lettering and [R.J.] Beedham cleared it for me.'[29] This must refer particularly to the extraordinary title-page, where he played more confidently and adventurously with the same Moyllus Alphabet.[30]

BHS seems to have given full rein to his imagination in the engravings. The images owed nothing to traditional Christian iconography, a matter of concern to some contemporary critics. However, a close examination reveals that every detail is related to the text, however personal the overall vision might appear. Conventional realism was not his goal.

The publication of *The Revelation of Saint John the Divine*, on 5 April 1933, coincided with the opening of an exhibition of BHS's wood-engravings at the Zwemmer Gallery in London. Even allowing for gallery hype there are indications in John Gould Fletcher's foreword to the catalogue that BHS's reputation was now firmly established: 'For this young man stands at the very head of the many artists who are producing wood engravings in England . . . he has now, as an engraver, reached full maturity.' He mentions BHS's acknowledged debt to Underwood and his school and goes on to say: 'Where Underwood himself is by temperament a cosmopolitan of the Renaissance type, Hughes-Stanton is in spirit less cosmopolitan than English. There is always about his work a peculiar lyrical quality that makes it akin to Blake, to Turner or to Augustus John. This lyrical quality has its affinities with literature as well as with decoration. As Stanton himself recently wrote to the author of this foreword: "I do seem to get my imagination from words, and even when I am doing things of my own, it is as if it comes to me in words like a poem, and I put it into forms. All the time that I work, I seem to feel word rhythms, and that is why I like to work to books.'''

THE HONOUR OF YOUR COMPANY IS
REQUESTED AT THE PRIVATE VIEW ON
WEDNESDAY   APRIL 5   1933
OF AN EXHIBITION OF THE
WOOD   ENGRAVINGS
OF
BLAIR HUGHES - STANTON
INCLUDING THOSE ENGRAVED FOR
THE   REVELATION   OF   SAINT   JOHN
PUBLISHED BY
THE GREGYNOG PRESS
AT THE
ZWEMMER   GALLERY
26 LITCHFIELD STREET, CHARING CROSS RD. W.C.2
APRIL 5 TO APRIL 29   10 A.M. TO 6 P.M.

Zwemmer Gallery Invitation, 1933

These remarks were often quoted back at BHS in the next half century. They were not however meant to be taken too literally and he was irritated when pushed to elaborate. He felt that explanations were mostly superfluous and that the work should be allowed to speak for itself.

By the time BHS had left the Press in September 1933, he had designed and illustrated two more books: *Four Poems* (1933) by John Milton and *The Lamentations of Jeremiah* (1934). The former work was completed in January but not published until October. The poems, namely 'L'Allegro', 'Il Penseroso', 'Arcades' and 'Lycidas', again chosen principally as a vehicle for the engravings, are printed in Gill's Perpetua type. There was no problem this time with the italics. The quality of the typography is again, and predictably, inferior to that of the engravings, which perhaps intentionally distract the attention. The special binding with its geometric design of gilt-outlined panels variously crushed or plain, left empty or tooled with fine lines or cross-hatching in blind is surprisingly lifeless compared with the nymph blocked in blind on the red Hermitage calf of the ordinary binding.

The exuberant images of frolicking nymphs and shepherds are almost certainly a celebration of the unconventional, unrestrained and now unfettered love affair between BHS and Ida Graves — a subject soon to be given the awesome and almost gruesome full treatment in their own

vi, 123–7
128–32

148–53 *Epithalamion*. In fact, her image as Woman permeated and dominated all his work from as early as 1931 until the War.

The same female figure appears again, disguised this time as the
128–32 Daughter(s) of Zion, in *The Lamentations of Jeremiah*. BHS again arranged the format with its five full-page chapter openings and its other smaller and rather less successful engravings cut to fit the text, which was set in Baskerville italic. The engraved title-page is a display of incredible skill. He has dared to italicise and stretch his by now familiar Moyllus alphabet — an indication, if any were needed, of his ever-increasing self-confidence. The chapter titles and initial letters were also engraved and printed in a mixture of blue and black, the blue adding to rather than relieving the deliberately funereal quality. Harrop quotes a review by Bernard Newdigate in *The London Mercury* in which he expressed admiration for the skill of the engravings but considered that 'neither these nor any other engraved pictures can convey the sense of utter desolation borne by the bible text.'[31]

These engravings mark a shift in style — away from the voluptuous translucence of *The Revelation* to a harsher angularity, with the return of the strong black silhouette. Was this the result of the nature of the work, the natural progression of his development, current fashion, or a combination of the three? Whatever the precise answer to that question BHS was gradually to develop this tendency to the extremes of surrealism and abstraction, once freed from the restraints imposed on him at Gregynog.

The spectacular binding for the fifteen specials of *The Lamentations* now also look very much of the period (although at the time, his work was considered extremely, excessively, *avant garde*). The paper pattern for the binding, still in the safe at Gregynog, shows that although by now confident, not to say audacious, in his design and in the means to achieve it, he still deferred to Fisher on certain technical points: 'Lettering as fits best'; 'Bands to be genuine or false as Mr Fisher thinks best and additional flat invisible bands if necessary. Bands to protrude as far and sharply as possible'; and even 'Design can repeat in reverse on back or back can be plain as considered best from time or economy point of view.' The book was to be covered in a brown black like the ink on the pages and inlaid with blue Hermitage calf and white levant. The ordinary copies, with the blind-blocked titling and GG press device superimposed on a cross, are a relatively sombre affair.

The above reference to economy is a reflection of the effects of the depression. So too was the Board's decision to restrict the number of copies to 175. An edition of 250 had, however, already been printed.[32] The reference to time reflects the fact that as George Fisher was solely responsible for the finishing of the specials, he was always at least two years behind publication. This state of affairs did not help sales which were already difficult enough at that time.[33]

It was hardly the moment therefore that BHS would have chosen to leave the subsidised cocoon of Gregynog to set up his own press. But the end, as has been related elsewhere, was not entirely unexpected.[34] Not long after Gertrude's departure for London early in 1932 Ida joined BHS at Gregynog. This unconventional step outraged the highly conventional directors of the Press Board, who in May sought the termination of his contract. The reputation of the Press was at stake not to mention the tranquility of Tregynon, the village where most of the Press workers lived. Gwen Davies, in a letter to T.J., displays the quandary of the Board: 'We don't want to lose Hughes-Stanton. He is one of our chief assets but we can't allow him to do *just anything* he likes. But we mustn't do things in a hurry. I think Stanton has had a fright. W.J. [Burdon Evans] gave him a "talking to" and perhaps he will send the lady away — we felt bound to protest.'[35] The directors were reluctant to dispense with his services until *The Revelation* was completed, and as BHS refused to go without compensation, he held on to his post. 'Evidently Stanton has us in a cleft stick.'[36]

His cohabitation offended not only the Board but also his friend McCance, who confided his worries to Stanley Morison. They were both shocked that the Board was prepared to tolerate the affair for as long as it was financially convenient.[37] He also wrote to Gertrude in June, noting that BHS was already showing a degree of irritability towards Ida: '. . . I do not feel any real vital love of two young people, none of the enthusiastic fresh wonder of the love of two people who are living in a new world. Already it seems to me a fixed static love of acceptance and lack of surprise or revelation. There is a certain amount of adulation and idolatory but not a deep realistic revealing contact. But this is only a very personal reaction on my part.'[38]

Two new temporary contracts, agreed in September and December 1932, allowed BHS to remain at the Press until the following September to complete the work in hand. In the search for successors to BHS and McCance the Press Board was keen to avoid similar problems in the future. T.J. wrote to his daughter Eirene: '. . . it is probable that at the end of their agreements (September 1933) we'll close the McCance-Stanton chapter and begin Chapter III with an expert typographer and no artists on the spot, as they are so hard to handle.'[39]

Readers are again referred to Dorothy Harrop's *The Gregynog Press* for the results of this policy as we close the Gregynog chapter of BHS's life. He did not, however, completely sever his links with the press and did one frontispiece engraving ('Saved' for *Gweledigaetheu y Bardd Cwsc*, 1940) and three special binding designs (for *The Star of Seville*, 1935; *Caelica*, 1937; and *The Lovers of Teruel*, 1938) after his departure.

157

4

INDEPENDENCE

1933–1939

In the Christmas holidays of 1932 BHS and Ida went to London. There they met the writer Arthur Calder-Marshall, who became a close and lifelong friend of BHS, and who has kindly written this account of their meeting and of the circles in which they moved:

I first met Blair and Ida at Epstein's studio in late December 1932 on a Sunday afternoon.

The night before . . . I had strolled into the Café Royal, hoping to meet someone I knew and Laz [Aaronson] was the only one . . . He listened sympathetically to my excitement at having just heard that Jonathan Cape had just accepted my second novel *About Levy* and when I expressed my admiration for the portrait busts of Jacob Epstein and bewilderment at his 'Genesis', he invited me to come to Epstein's open Sunday tea, meet the great man and see the controversial sculpture, instead of judging by the photographs in the press.

I was enormously impressed by the great studio and the quiet strength and unflamboyance of Epstein himself. Of 'Genesis' I was not sure. It needed to be seen in a more open setting: whereas the portrait busts were so intimate one wanted to stroke them.

It was a very Jewish gathering, and I was more conscious of Epstein being a Jew than of his being an artist. Apart from Laz, who was, like Humbert Wolfe, a civil servant in the Ministry of Labour first and only poet second, there were Professor Jack Isaacs[1], a clever Whitechapel boy made good as English Lit. scholar, and Dr Claude Elman, who had sprung from the same background to become a general practitioner. Catalysis led me to the only other gentiles, BHS and Ida Graves . . . . We got on so well together that we left Epstein's together and since it was only 6.30, we walked from Kensington to Piccadilly Circus to kill time before the Café Royal opened.

During that walk and the three hours we spent drinking and talking until the café was closed, we became such friends that it seemed tragic that next morning I had to go to Worthing to spend Christmas with my parents . . . . How did they strike me that first meeting?

Well, firstly that they were passionately in love and were proud to show it, even though they were both married . . . . Like D. H. Lawrence and Frieda.[2]

I had been a blind worshipper of Lawrence. I still thought him the greatest of English writers, at his best: though I was becoming critical of his bullying and ranting. I was fascinated by two people who were living their lives according to the gospel of D.H.L. It showed a magnificent contempt for THEM, (THEY being the smug, the rich, the conventional, the philistine, etc.). That was the second bond.[3]

The third was that they both accepted me not as an usher teaching miserably at a third rate public school, but as a writer, a fellow artist engaged in the war against THEM.

Blair . . . found it as difficult to express himself in words as he found it easy to express himself pictorially. He was as inarticulate as Stan Laurel, and as clever. I suffered from a similar limitation. I didn't know what I wanted to say until I'd written it down. This made our conversation stimulatingly fatuous. But one thing did emerge. Blair wanted to illustrate what I wrote . . . .

. . . . I had published only one novel (*Two of a Kind*, which I realised was so amateur I should have suppressed it). They accepted my own judgement that the second, *About Levy*, was worth publishing: and Blair suggested that he might design a jacket, if Jonathan Cape agreed.   122

In the event Cape liked the engravings so much that they used the larger one from the front of the jacket as the frontispiece and the smaller one from the spine on the title-page. The rather prominent attribution 'JACKET AND FRONTISPIECE BY BLAIR HUGHES-STANTON' on the spine of the jacket, now even more prominent as the red of the author's name has faded, may have been designed to increase sales for the unknown writer. To judge by the notices, however, the novel was a literary success. Graham Greene wrote in *The Spectator*, 'No other novel I have read this year has interested or excited me more; and a second reading has only confirmed my impression of its importance.'

The engravings for *About Levy*, published in 1933, are, not surprisingly, very similar in feel to those for *The Ship of Death* (1933), a collection of   133–7 poems by D. H. Lawrence, published by Martin Secker that same year. Much about this latter book, such as the simple binding of brick-red paper covered boards with a black linen spine suggests that BHS had a hand in its design. He told me that after the publication of *Birds, Beasts and Flowers* (1930), which Lawrence had liked, they were going to collaborate on another volume.[4] Lawrence's death intervened, but BHS and Ida put together this selection from the writer's *Last Poems*.[5] The title-page reads:

THE SHIP OF DEATH AND OTHER POEMS
BY D. H. LAWRENCE WITH WOOD
ENGRAVINGS BY BLAIR HUGHES-STANTON

This arrangement does more than hint that the engravings are not to be regarded as a subsidiary element of the book. Arthur Calder-Marshall even considers that 'the illustrations enhance the quality of Lawrence's poems.'[6]

The engravings in *The Ship of Death* retain the harsher style of *The Lamentations*, although they are less remote and more personal. The anguish of the poems permeates them. It has already been noted how BHS recorded his sense of bereavement at Lawrence's death in 'A Man Died' in 1931. He now illustrated the personal poems on death in this collection with a thin, bearded figure which is again patently Lawrence himself. Inspired as he was by Lawrence's views on death and by his death itself, he was even more impressed by his utterances on morality and life. Having spent over a year being vilified for 'living in sin', it is no wonder that he identified with such lines as: 'There is no such thing as sin./There is only life and anti-life.'[7] and: 'And life is for delight, and bliss'.[8]

The attempt to put this philosophy into practice not surprisingly caused much trouble, disappointment and unhappiness both for himself and for his families. To Lawrence's other preoccupations, as revealed in these poems, such as his yearning for perfect sex, male friendship and his passionate sympathy for the shackled workers of the machine age, BHS responded almost literally in his work and life. For the argumentative but not reliably articulate BHS, who used to say that he had 'plenty of faith but no belief', it was reassuring to find a literary champion more daring and shocking than himself. It was amusing, for example, for me to find that the engraving of whales, one of BHS's most admired works (especially by people who find his figures too disturbing and explicit) accompanies in *The Ship of Death* a poem, 'Whales Weep Not', which is in fact an explicit celebration of the apparently enviable sex-life of the said huge mammals.[9]

The Ship of Death, then, although not a rarified production in the Gregynog mould, was a book of seminal importance in the life and work of Blair Hughes-Stanton.

Blair Hughes-Stanton, in the mid thirties

148–53   *Epithalamion* (1934), which followed, was intended to be the ultimate embodiment of his idea of the perfect collaboration between writer and artist. This idea was incorporated into the very name of his new press, The

Gemini Press, which he set up himself, with the financial and moral support of Robert Sainsbury. It was symbolised in the press device, II.[10] In the 'Intimation' in the original prospectus he wrote:

I have founded the Gemini Press to be able, when occasion arises and unhampered by any outside prejudices, to make books in which there is a real fusion between contemporary writer and artist, and where possible a definite collaboration from the start, so that the book is integral and not a decorated or illustrated vehicle of text. By personal printing and publishing it will be economic to produce at a reasonable price, yet with fine hand craftsmanship, experimental work of this kind which could not reach the public otherwise.

Epithalamion, the first volume, is a poem of extreme beauty and grandeur in twenty three stanzas, dedication and envoi; the twenty three page engravings were cut as the poem progressed, a drawing occasionally directing it. Hand set and printed by myself in 24 pt. Blado italic the edition is limited to 50 signed copies on hand made Japanese Vellum, half bound to my design in French Levant Morocco and leather edged etui by Sangorski and Sutcliffe, priced £5 5s, and 280 copies, 30 are not for sale, on Basingwerk Parchment, paper boards and boxed, priced 30/–.

Ida Graves, in the mid thirties

Epithalamion, 'A Poem by Ida Graves with Associate Wood-Engraving by Blair Hughes-Stanton', is dated at the end of the text: Tregynon 1933. If the prospectus is to be believed, BHS must have completed all the

D

engravings before leaving the Gregynog Press. Some of the later engravings, however, seem to be more in the style of work which he certainly did in 1934. Perhaps, though, they were the precursors of that work. The move to Valley Farm Cottage in Higham, Essex, the birth of his son Corin (28 November 1933), the installation in the barn of the big Columbian press that Robert Sainsbury had bought for him, cannot have left much time for engraving that autumn, even allowing for the fact that he engraved extremely quickly. Be that as it may, the 'comping' had started by mid-February 1934, a slight delay resulting from his having 'forgotten the lay of the case'.[11] The colophon states that the printing was completed on the 30 June 1934. The dates in the notebook where he recorded all expenditure on the book confirm this schedule. This record makes interesting reading:

Feb.	14	Messrs Arnold Foster (trial paper)		6	7
Feb.	16	Mander Bros. ink		6	6
		Sidney Rourke & Co. (art paper boards)	2	4	11
Feb.	19	Spalding and Hodge, interleaving paper			
		overlay paper	2	3	0
Feb.	20	Crompton Bros. (Jap Vellum)		4	4½
Feb.	22	Spalding Hodge, carriage paper		2	6
Feb.	26	Carriage paper, Spalding Hodge		1	3
Apr.	10	Grosvenor Chater Basingwerk Parchment	11	0	10
Apr.	12	Crompton Bros. (Jap Vellum 1 Ream)	16	5	5
April		German ink for engravings		16	0
July		,, ,, ,, ,,		16	0
May	1	Extra 125 Vellum	3	19	11
Sep.	27	Vellum End Paper	1	15	10
,,	,,	Wiggins Teape Alex Pirie Cover paper	2	10	2
Aug.		Canson Montgolfier Cover paper	4	6	0
Mar.	9	Mansell and Co. Bookbinders	6	1	9
,,		Sangorski and Sutcliffe	17	6	9
Feb.		1 Copy of Special	1	5	0
Total			71	12	9½

The same notebook records the sales of *Epithalamion*. Thanks to the economic climate only half of the fifty specials and 175 of the 300 ordinary copies were disposed of, either sold or given as presents or review copies. They were bound as required.[12] Leading booksellers such as Myers, Truslove and Hanson, Zwemmer, Miller and Gill, Bumpus and Foyles took copies of both kinds on sale or return — and generally sold them. BHS was not a great salesman and therefore it is not surprising that direct sales did not extend far beyond the circle of their friends.

Notable among the direct purchasers of the specials were Alan and Robert Sainsbury (who were both valued friends and patrons), Herbert Marks (Ida's husband, whose *Pastoral, or Virtue Requited* was to be the next Gemini Press publication), and Christopher Sandford (whose *Primeval Gods*, with engravings by BHS had just been published, and who, as the new owner of the Golden Cockerel Press, was negotiating terms for engravings for two other books for that press). 'HRH' (George V) and the British Museum accounted for another two of the specials.

Among the buyers of the ordinary copies were the artists Lett Haines, who lived nearby in Higham, Ivon Hitchens, Jacob Epstein and Marion Stancioff (née Mitchell, from Underwood School days). Others went to Douglas Cleverdon, The Halcyon Press, John Gould Fletcher, whose appreciative effusions on BHS are quoted above, and Arthur Calder-Marshall. Review copies went to most of the newspapers. A copy was given to Pearl Binder 'for Russia' and another to the Spanish Aid Sale — thereby giving an indication of BHS's political inclinations. Sir Herbert, BHS's father, bought a few copies. This was a late acknowledgement of the talents of his son, whose work he had failed to understand.

Epithalamion, meaning nuptial song or poem in praise of the bride and groom, is a sequence of sexual imagery and symbolism, a celebration of love, consummation and conception. For the artist and poet, however, marriage was out of the question, even though Gertrude had divorced Blair, because Ida's marriage to Herbert Marks (a chartered accountant who numbered several synagogues amongst his clients), could not be dissolved without his ruin. Having left Ida for Isobel Powys and having removed their children, Anna and Anthony, Marks gave her maintenance on condition that she took the whole blame for the separation.[13]

Epithalamion was not Ida's first publication. *The China Cupboard and Other Poems*, No. 5 in the Hogarth Living Poets Series, had been published by the Hogarth Press in 1929, with a cover design by Vanessa Bell. In addition, various stanzas of *Epithalamion* itself had previously appeared in *Life and Letters*.[14]

While printing *Epithalamion* BHS had engraved small blocks for Christopher Sandford's *Primeval Gods*, published by the Sandfords' own Boar's Head Press after Faber and Faber had refused to issue it. David Chambers, in his article on the Boar's Head and Golden Hours Presses states that the BHS engravings add 'much more to the volume than publication by Faber & Faber could have done . . . . Placed at the head of the various poems they add enormously to the impact of the book, the naked figures re-echoing Sandford's poetry, aptly described by *The Times* as "appropriate to nudist ecstasy . . . ecstatic hymning of a renovated procreative impulse". Sandford, himself, said it was much influenced by D. H. Lawrence.'[15] 140–41

BHS and Ida offered literary as well as typographical suggestions. They thought that he should drop the foreword and allow the poems to stand on their own. They disliked the title, *Primeval Call*, and suggested *There are Gods* or *To New Gods* instead. Obviously a compromise was reached. Sandford also seems to have heeded BHS's advice not to use italic.[16]

At the same time BHS was working on two other projects with Christopher Sandford in his capacity as the new owner of the Golden Cockerel Press: *A Crime against Cania* (1934), by Arthur Calder-Marshall, the ninth 146–7 in the Golden Cockerel Series of first editions by contemporary authors; and *Ecclesiastes, or The Preacher*, the hundredth book printed by the Golden Cockerel Press. The colophons of both books state that they were completed on 15 October 1934, the thirteenth anniversary of the foundation of the Press.

In a letter to the author, Arthur Calder-Marshall wrote about the genesis of *A Crime against Cania*: 'Blair urged me to write poems, but I realised that any talent I had was for prose . . . . and it was specially for Blair that I wrote *A Crime against Cania* . . . the text was not worthy of the illustrator . . . . He gave it a pictorial dimension which condensed into two dimensions the gist of what I needed many pages to set out. He was my idea of a perfect illustrator.'[17] The four small wood-engravings certainly seem to capture the threatening atmosphere of the novel set in Terma, a town lying in the shadow of Cania, a smoking volcano.

The engravings show more than a hint of the influence of the Surrealist movement. They are again cut more openly to suit the quality of the Batchelor paper, making more use of contrasting black and white instead of playing with textured greys. Freed from displaying sheer virtuosity he appears to have been more bold with the design of the images as a whole — not that the engravings are necessarily more successful for this liberation, but are an interesting and obviously necessary development after the isolation and constraints of Gregynog.

143–5 This trend is also to be seen in the engravings for *Ecclesiastes* and even more so in his numerous pen and watercolour sketches and in his colour engravings. After leaving Gregynog, where he had concentrated solely on engraving for books and had only been *thinking* about painting, he found that when he started to paint again he was painting exactly as he had in the late twenties. He told Norman Ackroyd: 'You've got to practise something, you can't just think about it and do it.'[18] The only oils that remain from the years 1933–35 are two very strange copies in brown, blue and black of engravings from *Epithalamion*. Luckily he realised that this was not a productive approach and in 1934 turned to watercolour as a way of getting back into colour and a non-illustrative frame of mind. The 1934 watercolours fall into two groups: the first a bizarre set of surrealist figures in bare mountainous landscapes; and the second an exuberant set of free, calligraphic, Picasso-esque figures with horses. By 1935 the themes are less contrived, more natural and immediate, with titles like 'Nude on a Couch', 'Artist and Model' and 'Spring Girl'.

More time, care and attention must have gone into the four colour engravings, 'The Shore', 'The Rock', 'Horizon' and 'Composition'. These relatively large prints were engraved on pear wood end-grain, and are printed in three colours, two of them without the use of a black key-block. The first one, 'The Shore', which does include black as one of the colours is closely related in style to the illustrations for *Ecclesiastes*. The recumbent female printed in black with minimal engraved detail is identical to her counterpart in the book, as is the beckoning male, over-printed in mushroom brown, in all his harsh and precise anatomical detail, except for the removal of his beard. Two of the other engravings are much more subdued, printed in paler, smoky colours without the black. Like most of BHS's non-commissioned work there appears to be a strong autobiographical dimension. These two are not particularly happy pictures. There is an atmosphere of confusion and despair in the male as in 'The Maze' and 'The   170 Fugitive' of the late twenties. In 'The Rock' he stands arms raised in mournful desperation in the barren landscape of surrealist rocks with Woman out of reach on a monolithic pedestal. What appears to be a hole in the rock turns out on closer inspection to be a curled up foetus, which may be the clue to the cause of all the trouble. In 'Horizon' the man is looking even more dejected, sitting on a rock with two females in the foreground, and a couple going off towards two anthropomorphic rocks on the horizon. Although these colour engravings helped the transition back to thinking in colour and to painting in oils, and although BHS himself was pleased with them, without the black much of the strength and impact is gone, which may explain why this experiment with colour wood-engraving was short-lived. By reinforcing what he must already have known, that wood-engraving, like etching, is an essentially black-and-white medium, he was now free to develop his style within the restrictions of the medium. This resulted in the striking series of black and white semi-abstract engravings produced in the years before the war.

While making these private adventures into colour during the years 1934–35, BHS was still busy fulfilling commissions for books before the market was strangled completely. In addition to *Epithalamion, Primeval Gods, Ecclesiastes* and *A Crime against Cania*, 1934 also saw the publication of three other works with engravings by BHS: *Elegies and Songs*, a   139 pamphlet of rather opaque poetry by John Mavrogordato, published by Cobden-Sanderson, bears a cover engraving of a frolicking female nude; *Tomorrow is a New Day*, subtitled *A Fantasy*, by T. O'B. Hubbard and   138 published by Lincoln Williams, has eight full-page engravings in an uncomfortable and uncharacteristic illustrative style; and *The Devil and*   142 *All*, by John Collier (who had first made his name with the publication in 1930 of *His Monkey Wife: or Married to a Chimp*), has a frontispiece of the Devil, BHS's only work for Francis Meynell's Nonesuch Press. [19]

With its large edition of 1,000 copies and its lively individual typography, *The Devil and All* is a typically eccentric product of the Nonesuch Press. Meynell himself wrote, '. . . we were the first to cater for a large, growing and unsatisfied interest in 'fine books' at less than the fine prices required by the great 'private presses' with their limits of two to four hundred copies and their rigid retention of a single style; whereas our limited editions went sometimes as high as 1,500 and there was a vast variety in our types, bindings, sizes.'[20] This rejection of the rarified, prohibitively expensive, often self-indulgent products of the private presses in favour of well-designed books 'that had a good reason for existing'[21] must have helped Nonesuch survive the depression when private presses went to the wall. Christopher Sandford at the Golden Cockerel Press used the same survival tactic of using Chiswick of which he was director, thereby economising on plant and manpower, and became a publisher of fine books rather than a private press owner in the strict sense.[22]

1935 was a desperate year financially. Commissions for books had completely dried up. A cover engraving for a B.B.C. pamphlet, *An Approach to Art* by Eric Newton, was the only one. That commission cannot have done much to supplement Ida's private income of £4 per week on which they had to live. In desperation BHS consented to print and illustrate *Pastoral, or Virtue Requited* by H.H.M. and publish it as the second book of his own Gemini Press. The mysterious author of this slim volume of sardonic verse was Ida's husband Herbert Marks. The four wood-engravings are raucous and purely illustrative, showing an almost deliberate lack of sympathy for the text. Such a commission must have been depressing, almost shameful, after the idealism of total cooperation and sympathy between author and artist expressed in the 'intimation' of *Epithalamion*. BHS's feelings on the subject are expressed in an undated letter which was sent with a copy of *Pastoral* to John Mavrogordato,

154–5

Dear Mavrogordato,
    This is not really very good if you don't like it send it back, its partly a job but may help to produce something of a more serious vein next year. I have just got some temporary teaching at Westminster if it can only be used as a stepping stone to something permanent it will be a big relief. This year has not been pleasant. We come to London to get another baby the end of November, perhaps I can see you then.[23]

Kristin was born on Christmas Day 1935. In January they moved into Weaver's House, a late mediaeval timber house in Stratford St Mary, Essex, which Ida had bought for £450. Its restoration from a plastered ruin required much of their time over the next few years. Furniture and carved wooden sculpture from BHS's father, who died in 1937, helped turn it into an exceptionally beautiful house, later to be featured in *Country Life*.[24]

BHS tended, however, to spend increasing amounts of time in London. As he mentioned to Mavrogordato, he was teaching life drawing at Westminster School of Art, which, under its dynamic principal Kirkland Jamieson, was an interesting place in the 1930s. Other staff included Bernard Meninsky, Mark Gertler, Ernest Tedarb, Clifford Webb, Tom Chadwick and Gertrude Hermes. BHS was a charismatic teacher, especially popular with women. Among his students was a very young Australian student, Anne Ross, who was to be his third wife — but neither of them were yet aware of that. He also taught in a London prison. When in London he stayed with Gertrude and the children and often also with Arthur and Ara Calder-Marshall in Bayswater and later at their flat in the old cinnamon warehouse in Rotherhithe, overlooking the Pool of London.

Having set the press up again in an out-building in the garden he continued with his own semi-abstract engravings in black and white and a series of related oil paintings, 'Myth I – Myth VI'. Commissions were still relatively unforthcoming. Two small jobs came from Gregynog in 1936: a frontispiece engraving, 'Saved', for the bilingual work *Gweledigaetheu y Bardd Cwsc: Visions of the Sleeping Bard*, by Ellis Wynne, not published until 1940; and a special binding design of pink vellum stars onlaid on to night blue levant morocco for *Caelica*, by Fulke Greville, Lord Brooke (the first book at the Press designed by James Wardrop) and published in 1937.

157

He also engraved twelve little headpieces, one for each month's recipes in the *National Mark Calendar of Cooking* (1936). 'The National Mark', the booklet explains, 'is a Government trade-mark and a sign of controlled quality. It means that National Mark food is good food, and not only good but the best of its kind, marketed under the supervision and control of the Ministry of Agriculture and Fisheries . . . . the food is our own country's food, produced in England and Wales by our own folk and all the better for it.'

156

BHS with Corin and Kristin, *c.* 1939

Robert Sainsbury asked him to print an edition of 50 copies of Abraham Lincoln's Gettysburg Address. Set in Blado Italic on Imperial sheets of Japanese Vellum they were bound in dark green leather and given to friends as Christmas presents. They represent the third and last publication from the short-lived Gemini Press.

In the remaining three years before the war BHS developed his series of personal engravings of semi-abstract figures. The deliberately vague and

similar titles have led to confusion over the years, for the artist himself not
172   to mention his collectors. 'Holy Family', alternatively titled 'Composition', engraved in 1935, is clearly autobiographical with Woman/Ida

'Mother and Child',
Gemini Press Christmas Card, 1936

173   pregnant and breast-feeding and entwined with the Man/Blair. 'Creation',
also sometimes called 'Composition', engraved the following year, is much
175   more abstract, the figures barely discernable. 'Figures II' (which some-
174   times bewilderingly appears as 'Figures I'), and 'Two Figures (I)', 1937–
38, are a pair of well balanced images which demonstrate a retreat from
complete abstraction to a more comfortable distortion. The abstraction is
restricted to a functional role in the design rather than being allowed to

dominate and merely make a statement about itself. The scrolled Regency couch makes as strong an impact as the figures themselves and recurs in the later smaller engravings of 1938, 'Venus' ('Nude') and 'Conversation', 176; 177 which also show other furniture and more details of the interior of Weaver's House. A large block, variously titled 'Two Figures Vertical', 'Two 46 Figures' and 'Composition', displays a strength and dynamism whose further development was cruelly curtailed by the war.

At this stage BHS must have been aware and proud of his reputation and influence which prompted the engraver Clare Leighton to remark: 'Blair Hughes-Stanton is paying the price of his brilliance by having many imitators, till a school of fantastic, obscure mysticism threatens to swamp the individualism of English engraving.'[25] A more positive recognition of his talents as a wood-engraver was his selection, in 1938, as one of a very few artists chosen to represent Britain in Venice at the 21st International Biennale Exhibition of Fine Arts. The other artists were Jacob Epstein, Paul Nash, Matthew Smith, Stanley Spencer, Christopher Wood, Stanley Anderson and a group of eighteenth and nineteenth century masters. BHS was awarded the International Prize.

The parallel oil paintings of this period show a similar ease with subject matter and technique. Pale paint is scored to a darker under-surface so that the image is, in effect, engraved. Other colours are then superimposed. In his watercolours he used sharp pen and ink lines with the pale pastel shades to achieve the same hatched effect.

Beach holidays in the south of France were the main source of inspiration for the watercolours. In 1938 they went to Cassis with Mark Gertler and his wife Marjorie. Ida relates that Gertler was very silent and moody. He was particularly jealous when his wife painted. Ida would go to their digs, and keep watch at the window and warn her of his approach, so that she could hide her canvas, clear the paint and open doors and windows to clear the smell of turps. Ida herself was a victim of similar behaviour from BHS. 'Why are men so often jealous of their wives' talents? Gertler v. Marjorie (Paint); Blair v. me (sculpture, writing); Meninsky stopped Nora's stage dancing, and so on.'[26]

The following year they went again, this time with Alan Sainsbury, who had arranged to meet Babette, the young French woman who was later to become his wife. In the house where they stayed in St Raphael there was only one bedroom. BHS built a double bed for the lovers in the sitting room. Babette was amazed at the ferocity with which BHS and Ida argued and was confused on the first night at the sight of BHS emerging from the bedroom with a pillow and a blanket. They were, however, at the same time capable of great wit, charm and flirtation in the circle of writers and artists who spent the summer there.[27] The love for which they had braved so much was now mixed with a fair quantity of hate.

46   'Two Figures Vertical', 1938 (reduced from 15⅝ × 10¾ in)

5

THE WAR

1939–1945

The outbreak of the Second World War prevented any immediate resolution of the problems in BHS and Ida's relationship. BHS applied to join the Home Guard but was rejected on the grounds that he was a communist.[1] His ambition to become a War Artist was thwarted as his work was judged too pornographic.[2] In August 1940, however, he was appointed to an Emergency in the Royal Engineers Regular Army and a month later joined the Camouflage Training and Development Centre of the Royal Engineers at Farnham Castle.[3] There he was appointed a Staff Lieutenant and was trained by Major Richard Buckley. His fellow camoufleurs were a motley bunch, some only there for lack of any other obvious place for them to go, as David Fisher has described in his book on Jasper Maskelyne:

Besides the magician Maskelyne, the group included Victor Stiebel, a well-known couturier, painters Blair Hughes-Stanton, Edward Seago, Frederick Gore and Julian Trevelyan, designers Steven Sykes, James Gardner and Ashley Havingdon, sculptor John Codner, Oxford don Francis Knox, at forty-two the oldest recruit and an animal-camouflage expert, circus manager Donald Kingsley, zoologist Hugh Cott, art expert Fred Mayor, who decorated his room at the Castle with Rouaults and Matisses from his London gallery, and Jack Keefer, a West End set designer. Among their other classmates were a restorer of religious art, an electrician, two stained-glass artisans, a magazine editor, a *Punch* cartoonist and a Surrealist poet.[4]

After training BHS was tranferred to the large army base at Aldershot before being drafted to the Middle East. In November 1940 he was appointed General Staff Officer III (Camouflage Cyrenaica) and later, in February 1941, was posted as a Temporary Captain to HQ Abassia Royal Armoured Corps.[5] From Alexandria they sailed to Greece. At the end of that disastrous expedition he was not evacuated and was taken prisoner.

On Friday 2 May 1941 in the temporary P.O.W. camp at Corinth he very nearly lost his life. Edward Howell, a fellow *grand blessé*, explains how it happened: 'Conditions had been bad. There had been a good deal of shooting. Atrocity stories from Crete were circulating among the German guards. Until they were disproved, they were an excuse for reprisals. Blair had gone too near the wire to pick up an orange thrown in by a Greek civilian. The guard had shot him'.[6] The New Zealand doctor, John Borrie, who treated him takes up the story: 'In his dirty, blood-stained uniform, Captain Hughes-Stanton lay pale and shocked. He was conscious, his face swathed in bandages . . . . The bullet had entered the neck on the left, an inch below the angle of the jaw; the exit wound — puffy and gaping — was over the right cheek. Neck, throat, right upper jaw and maxillary antrum had all been perforated. I marvelled that he still lived, for his carotid arteries must have been grazed. We rebandaged him, gave him morphine and carried him to the Ionian Palace Hospital. Later, Slater protested to the Herr Kommandant of Corinth, but he was told only that "The guard had obeyed orders and done his duty"'.[7] Edward Howell, a pilot who had lost his arms, was in hospital with BHS: 'His face and mouth were a mess. And his jaws were wired together so that he could not speak properly or eat at all. He had to be fed on liquids for months. One of the familiar sights of the ward was Blair mashing up some fruit till it would pass through his teeth. He was very good to me. He supplied me with water at regular intervals for days and weeks, and he wrote my letters for me . . . . Through him, I began to realise my surroundings. He described the set-up. We were in a prison-camp on the outskirts of Athens. The hospital building had been a school. It was a huge, modern, white concrete building high on the hillside between Piraeus and Athens. The district was called Kokinia.' The hospital was run by an Australian doctor. It was very cramped with far more than 1,000 injured and food was scarce.[8]

BHS made drawings of his fellow inmates in the prison hospital with materials which Doctor Borrie had managed to procure 'for their small, vigorous Athenian School of Art'.[9] Only some of these drawings survived his subsequent moves through other camps before repatriation.

Prisoner of War No. 23805 was transferred to a transit camp in Germany — Stalag VIII B — in November 1941. There were still problems with the hole through his face and a tooth had to be removed. He had had no mail for months in Athens. Food was scarce and clothing inadequate for the cold weather. Rumours circulated about a move to an officers' camp — an outbreak of typhus, it later transpired, was the cause of the delay. They were isolated from other news. Boredom was the greatest enemy.[10]

The move in February 1942 to Offizierlager IX A/H, when it came, was disappointing. 'We have just had an influx of Senior Officers and lost a number of Air Force lads. The latter were very cheery and we hoped we would remain with them. The former have made the whole place rather crowded. I assist running the canteen and have started to do a bit of drawing in the mornings. So time will pass I hope quickly.'[11] He wrote that it was a disgrace that the *grand blessés* were kept for so long in such an overcrowded and inadequate place in defiance of the convention.[12] A certain amount of optimism appeared in the Spring when the trees started to bud and he was well and whole again. 'The country is quite pretty round here. Hills with larch and fir trees. We live in an old school house and its buildings with a small river full of ducks and geese on one side with the village street and timber houses beyond. The other side is barbed wire then the gardens where I have got a plot and work at it a couple of hours a day. But it is still cold at nights and things grow very slowly . . . I run an Art class here, mostly Colonels and Majors, but there is no one really interested in or understanding of modern painting. I feel very lonely sometimes, but get on generally well.'[13] By June the garden was growing but BHS found it difficult to regain weight and strength. He did not have enough energy to concentrate on his work but continued with his elderly Colonels and Majors, 'who want slick methods for watercolour painting, not my line, but they are grateful for help. I do colour schemes for the Brigadier's tapestry work. This I find exciting. May start myself when winter comes.'[14]

Captain Blair Hughes-Stanton, *c.* 1942/3

Although too unfit to contemplate escaping himself BHS did participate in escape work, as a result of which two managed to get out. The digging and diposal of earth by means of cocoa tins from food parcels was so efficient that even when the plan was betrayed the Germans took two weeks to find the entrance to the tunnel. BHS used his engraving skills to forge passes and used potatoes as rubber stamps. He also gave the escapees his compass, which he had managed to smuggle from camp to camp in his armpit.[15]

Rumours of repatriation came and went. Gertrude managed to get through parcels of cigarettes but BHS could provide little money as he received no marriage or childrens' allowance, being divorced from one wife and not married to the other. In October he was moved to yet another camp, yet worse than the last, Offizierlager IX A/Z. Although reconciled to a long wait after recurrent disappointments concerning repatriation BHS now found it impossible to work. 'I am afraid I've done no work as I'm in a room with 40 others and so get little peace and quiet. But I make a few notes and store up a lot, so that if I feel I ever want to remember this life again I shall be able to, but I find very little that I wish to remember or record . . . . It's terrible the time one is wasting over this business and just when we both seemed to be getting started, let's hope there is some peace and quiet when it is all over.'[16]

A spell in hospital, Stammlager IX, in January 1943 provided a welcome change of scene. The rest and privacy enabled him to do a few drawings.[17] Back at Oflag there was worse overcrowding thanks to the arrival of 150 Americans. But as summer approached they could sit outside in the sun, a relief from the cramped interior.[18] By July a certain optimism that the war might soon be over seems to have led to a more positive approach to prison life. They started playing soft ball and set up a league for competing teams. BHS's team won the league and the championship. He was also involved in the theatre: 'I've been very hard worked the last month doing the sets for an amusing review, they have come off very well and everybody is pleased. I am also acting the part of a comic 'Arty' woman. We have Dress Rehearsal tonight and play on three nights next week.'[19] In August 1943 he was already preparing the décor for the Christmas show at the same time as hoping that they would not be there for it. BHS was repatriated at the end of the year and returned to Farnham Castle where he continued with camouflage work until the end of the war.

6

FINAL YEARS

1945–1981

After the war a much weakened BHS returned home to Stratford St Mary. The familiar village pub provided the inspiration for his first post-war drawings. In pen and ink, some with watercolours, they show the locals singing at the piano, having discussions, and playing cribbage and 'snookerette'.

Because of the post-war decline of the private presses there were no commissions for wood-engravings. In any case the shot through the head had seriously affected his three-dimensional vision and thereby his ability to work with such technical precision. Three books containing wood-engravings by BHS were published in the forties, but in all three cases the engravings had been done before the war. In the case of Ida's slim book, the long poem, *Mother and Child* (1942), published by the Fortune Press, she had   158 found and used as frontispiece the block of their 1934 Christmas card, entitled 'Charity', and two tiny blocks from *The Lovers' Song Book*, (1931). Although the child in the poem is male, the inspiration was in fact the poet's daughter, Kristin.[1] It was dedicated to Alan and Robert Sainsbury.

Similarly *Voices on the Green*, published by Michael Joseph in 1945 reproduces an old engraving, 'Joy Bells', engraved for a B.B.C. Christmas card in 1933. The ten half-page wood-engravings for *The Confessions of An*   159–60 *English Opium Eater* by Thomas de Quincey and published by the Folio Society in 1948 had been engraved as early as 1930 for the Australian artist Jack Lindsay's Fanfrolico Press, which had gone bankrupt. The second reset edition of 1963 was better printed in every way. BHS was impressed with the printing of the blocks considering their age.[2]

In his new illustrations BHS turned to other media. For *African Folk*   159 *Tales* (1946), by Yoti Lane, for example, he used scraperboard drawings which gave the effect of rather coarse wood-engravings. The blurb says: 'The drawings are in colour by Blair Hughes-Stanton, the famous engraver. They establish a new note for children's book illustrations. Here the forest, the jungle, the strange world of the mysterious dark continent come alive.' In fact the drawings are simply printed in black over various pale coloured grounds and were not the part of his *oeuvre* of which he was most proud. He also used scraperboard drawings for another collection of children's animal stories, *A Zoo in Your House*, published by Dennis Yates in 1951.

More delicate pencil drawings for *Sense and Sensibility*, published by the Avalon Press in 1949 were reproduced lithographically as were those for

Trollope's *The Eustace Diamonds*, published by the Oxford University Press in 1950. The writing on the dust-cover of the latter work states: 'The Oxford Illustrated Trollope is meant to meet the demand . . . for an edition of Trollope's principal novels in a larger format and type . . . . The illustrations are new, but, under the Art-Editorship of Mr. LYNTON LAMB, great care has been taken that the several artists keep their work in "period". The original illustrations — apart from those by Millais — have no great artistic merit, but have always been consulted for costume and furniture.' When the book was reissued in 1973, simultaneously in paperback and clothbound editions, the chapter headpieces were retained but the full-page drawings were omitted.

This miscellaneous collection is the sum total of BHS's commissioned work for the five years before he left Ida in February 1950. After the series of pub drawings his personal output was also slight except for a series of experimental drawings in pastel of the willow-lined River Stour near Weaver's House. These drawings, which started off in 1947 as pure landscapes in restrained blues and greens, were by 1949 peopled with parties of scantily clad young women, in more vibrant tones. An equally uncharacteristic abstract oil painting from this period has also recently come to light. A certain amount of time was taken up with his activities as a Parish Councillor, but most of his energies went into teaching. Teaching was a financial necessity — he taught drawing and wood-engraving at Colchester School of Art and later wood-engraving at St Martin's — but it was a drain on his physical resources which were seriously depleted after the years in the P.O.W. camps.

The break with Ida, although possibly contemplated for years, was sudden after a violent fight in which, after receiving a severe blow to her temple, she almost managed to strangle him with his tie. Ida's version of the build-up to this horrific situation has been described in detail in her novel *Elarna Cane*, written under the name of Affleck Graves, and published by Faber in 1956.

Before the war Ida had had to tolerate BHS's insistence that he should be allowed to have affairs in London — because he was an artist and because in any case they were not married. Her complaints were greeted with increased rage and accusations of madness. After the war when (somewhat hypocritically) put out by Ida's infidelity during the war, he took to visiting a woman in the same village the situation was intolerable. *Elarna Cane* revolves around her jealousy and impotence in the face of this infidelity and his additional infatuation with the eponymous young village girl whom they employed to do the cleaning — although he did not, as the book suggests, father a child by her.

A perfectionist himself, BHS was enraged by Ida's lack of housewifely skills, which, having been brought up in India with staff and servants, she had never been expected to acquire. Another of the main accusations against her was that she was too intellectual. Her persistent ailments were 'neurotic', 'psychosomatic' and 'imaginary'. Other bones of contention were the humiliation of being financially supported by a woman and, of course, creative competition. The fact that Ida loved him deeply, even though she no longer liked him, merely served to compound the problem.

After the final fight in February 1950 BHS, physically and emotionally wrecked, left Stratford St Mary and, after taking refuge once again with Gertrude in Chelsea for a while, went to live in the ground-floor flat of Cumberland House, on South Hill in Manningtree, Essex, some three miles downriver. The house was owned and the upper floors occupied by the typographer, illustrator and author John Lewis and his wife Griselda, with whom he often worked in partnership.

Anne Hughes-Stanton with Penelope, 1954

Later that year Anne Ross, who had been one of BHS's students at the Westminster before the war, and who was now a vivacious woman in her early thirties, returned from Australia. During the war she had served in camouflage and had also painted murals for the Australian Army and the American Army. After the war she had specialised in painting eccentric junk furniture. On her return to England a message was transmitted to BHS, through a friend of Gertrude's and through Gertrude herself, that she would like to attend his engraving class at St Martin's. This was arranged and she did several linocuts. In spite of BHS's fear of another involvement so soon, a relationship between them developed quickly and

E

as she left to catch the boat home in September he pursued her to Brighton and proposed in the Pavilion. After nine months she returned and they were married on 14 June 1952.

During her absence his time was to a great extent taken up with teaching: he retained his engraving class at St Martin's at the same time as taking up a new appointment to teach drawing at the Central School of Arts and Crafts, which he did not like as well but where the money was better. For a term he was teaching four days a week, which he regarded as a desperate, temporary measure, only undertaken to save money for his honeymoon. As a permanent arrangement such a commitment would, he knew, be death to him as an artist.

In the intervals between teaching, writing long, daily letters to Anne, helping Gertrude print her large linocuts, shopping for his rationed provisions and cooking (which he, like many artists, was very good at) he embarked on a series of 18 drawings in pen and watercolour, some quite large, inspired by Greek mythology and heroic saga. His sources were *The Gods of The Greeks* by C. Kerényi (Thames and Hudson, 1951) and the new translation of *The Iliad* by E. V. Rieu (Penguin, 1950). His letters to Anne reveal the difficulties and lack of confidence he had with some of these drawings, although others seemed to go well. There was the dilemma in December 1951, for example, over whether to paint or pen first: 'I think I shall paint because in that way one gets away from the linear design and finds a colour one. Then one can mass it with the ink. Trouble is before I paint I must bread it [i.e. erase with bread] and then I may find I lose a lot of drawing. All very difficult and complicated.'[3] With each drawing taking weeks because of the technique, by early February he was very depressed: 'I can't concentrate properly and be at a real high pitch of intensity and feel I am getting old, out of date, no ideas and generally missed the bus. I must do smaller experimental drawings. I'm a bit dried up I think or want to alter my technique'.[4] By the end of that February, when he was printing the editions of some recent colour prints, he had even lost confidence in his sense of colour. 'In fact I don't think I've got much of a colour sense and better go back to black and white or get a heavy German book all about it. Everyone seems to work on a theory and I don't know one so I better read it up. I expect I should disagree violently but that might help to form my own theory. At the moment I don't know really what colours to put together. I am afraid it's a side I've neglected but probably quite a good time to go into it when one is really convinced one's made a balls of it for thirty years.'[5] He was, however, excited and inspired by *The Iliad*, which, after several readings, was very real to him. Some of his battle scenes are extremely complex and imaginative. The trigger for this temporary *crise de confiance* was probably the rejection of his work by the Hanover Gallery and then the Redfern Gallery. He hated showing his work, especially when it was rejected, but was convinced that he would flower with success, and did manage to retain a certain amount of faith in himself and his work.

The Homeric Drawings, as he usually called them, were eventually shown at the Leicester Galleries in June 1954. Also included in that exhibition were 25 monotypes which celebrated the new union with Anne, to the extent of portraying the various stages of her pregnancy with me, Penelope, the first of their two daughters. I was born on 4 February 1954. Chloë was born the following year on 26 July. The 'Two Figures' theme is loaded with the same degree of cosmic significance as ever, as shown by titles such as 'Dawn' (an old favourite), 'The Eclipse' and 'The Cycle'. 'Happy Spirits' indicates at last that he was content. Anne had picked him up from the floor and had restored him to his old confident self. The monotype self-portrait which was included in the exhibition was presumably made specially for *Art News and Review* where it accompanied a piece about the exhibition.[6]

BHS with Chloë and Penelope, 1955

When I was four months old we moved down the hill to North House which overlooks the Stour estuary at Manningtree. BHS designed the extensive renovations and did much of the physical work himself, as he had done several times before. We lived frugally on his earnings from two days a week teaching drawing at the Central.

In 1955 began the collaboration with Lewis and Dorothy Allen of the Allen Press in California, which was to revive and prolong his career as an illustrator of books. Because of the small matter of the 6,000 miles distance between Manningtree and San Francisco, their collaboration was maintained largely by post. Indeed the five titles on which they worked produced a file of about 300 letters, now in the archives of the University of

California Library (Rare Books Division). In a letter to the author, Lewis 'Lew' Allen wrote:

Although we met several times in England and Paris, these were primarily 'gin and french' celebrations.

The Allen Press was established in 1939 to produce by hand de luxe limited editions; our library boasted several handsome books illustrated by Blair. When 161–3 we decided to do *The Wreck of the Golden Mary* by Charles Dickens and Wilkie Collins in 1955 (another significant collaboration), we asked Blair, with rare temerity, if he would consider engraving seven full-page illustrations. Because of his fame as a book artist, we held slight hope of an affirmative answer. Although we spoke, roughly, the same language, there was the barrier of 6,000 miles. So we were ecstatic when he agreed. Such was the genesis of a long and fruitful callaboration — which developed into an enduring family friendship.

Technically, I profited greatly, being introduced by Blair in the mystique of the wedding of heavy copper-plate oil and basic black ink; and the attributes and qualities of grays and colors. Blair wrote: 'I think any results I get which seem to you in any way exceptional is in the ink; it must be very thin (copper-plate oil and black ink) and still make solid coverage. There is no possibility of it affecting the paper as the ink is rolled so thinly that there is no more oil left on the paper than that carried by full-bodied inks. I'll get some of this etching oil for you next time I'm in London.' Patience and kindness![7]

Their next collaboration was *Youth* by Joseph Conrad, 1959. Again let us allow Allen to tell his own story:

For the illustrator, our English friend Blair Hughes-Stanton was the obvious choice. Never one to accomplish art work simply, he came up with eight nine-color engravings involving delicate register problems. Also, to complete a nine-color process within a printing time-span of one week, we had to develop a plan to do three colors with one impression. All this was necessary because we damp the handmade paper for printing — a highly desirable technique. So we had to keep the beautiful Richard de Bas paper damp for one week. It was a hot, dry summer. At the end of five days we were shocked to see black spots of fungi. A chemical company sent us insecticide powder to mix with the water used for damping the paper. Next week's run was clean, but I developed severe intestinal disorders which were diagnosed as mercury poisoning. The final answer: use a mask and rubber gloves when damping. Blair was always amazed at the summer heat generated in California, and rightly, was concerned about his blocks warping and splitting due to climatic changes.

The illustrations were produced by making zinc blocks from black stage proofs of BHS's progressively cut linocuts. He also sent over colour swatches for reference. That this method was not always easy to follow is revealed in one of Allen's letters: 'Next time it would help to have the sequence of color proofs: proof of block 2 on block 1; block 3 on # 1 and 2, and so on, through the 5th block.' In his commentary on the book in *The Allen Press Bibliography* Allen continues:

The engraved illustrations are spectacularly dramatic, enhanced by the beautiful (and tamed) French paper . . . . Directors of the Palace of the Legion of Honor Museum in San Francisco gave a special exhibition of those remarkable illustrations. [February — March 1960].

The binding of white 'parchment paper' is enlivened by some units from the illustrations. Unfortunately, the slip-cases were covered with blue Japanese paper (used also for endsheets) which proved to be too delicate.[9]

Complicated to print as Lewis Allen found the progressive blocks for *Youth* to be, they were as nothing compared with the large multicoloured linocuts BHS was producing on his own Columbian Press at the time.[10]

Blair Hughes-Stanton, in the sixties

This new burst of confidence and inspiration was based on nothing more complicated than the acquisition of a new pair of bifocal glasses, which were a great improvement on the depressingly inadequate ones that he had been wearing since the war. As many as thirteen printings were required per print. Most are stylised, semi-abstract views from his studio window which faced north over the River Stour, or from the shore outside North House with its uninterrupted sight of both the rising and the setting sun on the mud-flats. He also spent long hours in the summer rowing upriver in his duck-punt which he looked after with an understanding gained four decades before on the training ship. In 1960 he made a small block for John Mason's book on papermaking. Three huge blocks, 'The Rock', 'The Cove', and 'The Wave' were engraved after a rare family holiday to Cornwall. These large colour linocuts were a new and exciting departure, more in line with the current trends in printmaking. They were exhibited at successive Royal Academy Summer Exhibitions, at exhibitions of the London Group of which he was a member, and at numerous international exhibitions.

In September 1960, BHS with his friend Morris Kestelman, who was Head of Fine Arts at the Central, attended the Third International Congress of Artists in Vienna, at which the definition of an Original Print was agreed. This definition, 'with notes for the guidance of artists, dealers and purchasers in the UK' was issued by the UK National Committee of the International Association of Painters, Sculptors and Engravers on which BHS served in 1962 and 1963. They had also attended an earlier one of these conferences in Dubrovnik in 1957. Indeed BHS's involvement in the international promotion of wood-engraving went back to 1953, when as a representative of the Society of Wood Engravers he attended a meeting at which it was decided to organise an international exhibition of wood-engraving. He subsequently attended the exhibition, called Xylon I, held in Zurich in September 1953.[11]

164   The next Allen Press book, *The Beast in the Jungle*, by Henry James, was published in 1963.

We discussed the 'Beast' with Blair Hughes-Stanton first when our families were together in Paris in April 1961. From April 1962 through February 1963 each of us wrote forty lengthy letters discussing the text, basic approach and style. In addition we debated on the most desirable tones of gray for the primary wood engravings, colors to be used for the over-printed [lino] blocks, the 'mystery' of copper-plate oil as an ink mixing agent, the manifold problems of printing, and the machinations of the U.S.A. Customs office. (One of the wood engravings was slightly warped when received; Blair claimed that a postal clerk must have set the package too near the primus stove when preparing his four o'clock tea!)

The sixteen illustrations printed directly from the wood [and lino] in two colors are remarkable for their unique style and their subtle allegorical interpretation of the emotional problems confronting the main characters. Hughes-Stanton wrote in one letter: 'I feel the protagonist blocked by squares, and dominated by his shadow; she (the other principal character) is fluid and her shape is the egg; the Beast lurks in the eye or ego; and in the second block the line entangles him, or sometimes holds them together; but eventually they break.' This, we believe, is a perceptive interpretation of a text by an artist.

As for typography, the text type lines are flush on the outer margins only, a departure from the conventional — as was the entire book.

For the first time in our edition printing adventures, in the style of French *édition de luxe*, we offered a separate portfolio containing a set of artist's proofs. In our prospectus: "For those desiring the ultimate in rare book illustration, Blair Hughes-Stanton has personally hand-printed, in his studio in England, fifteen sets of his sixteen two-color engravings, using a 15 × 10 inch handmade Japanese paper . . ." The portfolios were constructed at our Press, in the same style and materials as the binding of the books, also with an acetate jacket.[12]

By the mid-sixties BHS was beginning to feel his age. There were no new commissions and the old rage that he knew was caused by disappointment was beginning to surface again. Gertrude's election as an Associate of the Royal Academy in 1963 did nothing to help his own self-esteem, although he was genuinely delighted for her. He does not appear to have produced any work in the years 1963–1967. Why? There were distractions which he could conveniently blame: he was incapacitated for a time in 1965 with broken ribs caused by a fall; and just as he was recovering Anne had to go to Australia to be with her dying father and then cope with the disposal of the estate, leaving him to look after his two daughters. When not working he never lapsed into idleness: he spent hours in the garden and drew the plans for Anne's cottage in Sussex which she had unexpectedly inherited from an aunt. His main work during this period was framing sets of engravings and all his oil paintings, some of which had been stored away, unseen for 40 years, for a major retrospective at the Whitechapel Gallery promised by Bryan Robertson for September 1969.[13] Robertson had visited Manningtree several times before and after Gertrude's retrospective in 1967. He was impressed with BHS's painting and encouraged him to devote all his time to it. This encouragement prompted him to continue his new series of large canvasses: two of seated nudes with disquieting staring eyes and four of bikini-clad (originally nude) figures on beaches, a favourite theme from the past. After Robertson's departure from the Whitechapel Gallery it was revealed that he had told the Trustees nothing about this exhibition and that his promises represented no more than a personal commitment.[14] BHS had had disappointments before but nothing on this scale. After finishing those paintings he never did another.

A time-consuming distraction from his own work was BHS's involvement in the design and renovation of a succession of terraced houses in Harwich that Anne had bought with a view to letting to provide an income after BHS had retired from teaching.

The Allens came up with another commission in 1970, namely *Genesis*. But his collapse of morale made it difficult for him to produce work satisfactory either to himself or to his collaborators. The book has been judged one of the least successful of the press, largely on account of the inappropriateness of the illustrations.[15] Lewis Allen himself writes about it in rather guarded terms, although he appears to stand by it and BHS's illustrations:

165

. . . *The Book of Genesis* . . . with twenty-four . . . full-page engravings, was one of the most difficult to resolve artistically. We started off with ideas of two- or three-color engravings, and other evanescent solutions. Finally, at a zinc-board meeting in Paris, we decided on classical one-color blocks — which proved to have the necessary primitive simplicity and strength. Sales were brisk: one California public library included our *Genesis* in an exhibition of "Banned Books". Ridiculous: Blair's nude figures merely portrayed Old Testament lustiness.'[16]

I can remember BHS struggling for months to achieve the right kind of images for *Genesis*, a book in which he would have revelled a few decades before. They were eventually engraved as large lino-blocks and were reduced from the proofs for the book. The size of the blocks is in itself an admission of the failing of his physical capabilities. Of the fading of his creative powers also he was only too well aware. In 1973 he managed one final three-colour lino-cut for the Allen Press's *Four Fictions*. The prospectus explains this ambitious project:

. . . a concise presentation of Literature, Book Arts & Crafts of England, France, United States, and Italy. The authors — Joseph Conrad, Gustave Flaubert, Henry James, and Luigi Pirandello – are among the preeminent fiction writers of the past century, and the stories and novelettes selected are typical of their best work. To complete the nationalistic picture, each author's fiction has been illustrated with a full-page engraving or drawing in three colors by a noted artist of his country, and printed on paper made in that country. Although the typefaces (set by hand) vary, chosen to suit the text, the typography was developed to give uniformity to the book as a whole.

To counterbalance this increasingly dismal picture of the artist at three score years and ten let me quote Lewis Allen one last time: 'During our collaboration of over twenty-years, we at The Allen Press were impressed with Blair's finely attuned artistic skill and patient cooperation, and his warm, witty, and philosophic personality.'[17]

For this was the side of BHS that most people saw. When he was no longer producing work of his own, he devoted all his remaining energies to teaching, never allowing his personal tiredness and lack of inspiration to diminish his encouragement of others. Indeed his contact with the young became vitally important to him. At the Central, where he taught for nearly 30 years, he was loved and admired by generations of students, who fought off numerous attempts by officialdom to retire him. One of his students, the sculptor Glynn Williams told me: 'Some people are life-enhancers and some people are life-detractors. Blair was a life-enhancer.'

He loathed committee meetings. His ability to see the ludicrousness of most committee decisions is shown in an incident when the entire Fine Art Staff at Central were discussing candidates for the position of Head of Fine Art. One very good candidate was rejected by the assembly because of his known liking for alcohol, a second because of his liking for women. At this point in the meeting BHS halted the proceedings: 'If I may summarise the situation so far: we have established that what we are looking for is a teetotal homosexual!'[18]

By contrast BHS took the technical side of his teaching extremely seriously. David Esslemont, a student in the seventies, said: 'The technical lessons we received were so important: how to hold the tool properly; how to roll the ink out properly, which enabled you to control the inking.'[19]

BHS and Norman Ackroyd, outside the Central, 1977
Photo: Ian Hessenberg

A colleague at Central, Norman Ackroyd, has observed the way that BHS seemed determined to hand on his skill:

In the mid-sixties he almost single handedly refused to allow the Central to scrap their unique collection of relief presses. He set them up in the corner of the life-room, put them all in working order, and started to impart to a growing number of students his immense know-how and experience. He had an almost instinctive need to pass on all he knew.

Throughout the seventies he was in great demand and received unequivocal support from students and staff against persistent attempts by administrators to sack him. It is typical of BHS that when the administrators finally gave up and said he could teach as long as he liked, he decided to retire the following year, at the age of 77.

Christopher Holladay, the engineer who specialises in repairing and maintaining printing presses, and who cares for most of the old presses in Britain, said, in 1982, that wherever he travels he can guarantee that where relief presses are well maintained and where studio practice is high and professional, then the artist in charge has at some time been in contact with BHS, It is significant that David Esslemont who studied under BHS is now, in 1991, Controller of the Gregynog Press, 60 years after his mentor.

His legacy is immense. The relief presses are still in place at the Central. Many of his former students are now practising professionally all over Britain and the world. His influence will be felt well into the next century.

His secret was, I think, a perfect mixture of fun and discipline and an ability to see certain things clearly. His was a philosophy of instinct rather than intellect. His contribution to teaching was as brilliant and indispensable as his contribution to British book production in the twentieth century.[20]

For several years in the seventies he also trekked across England to teach at Winchester School of Art for a day before his two days in London.

A succession of exhibitions in the seventies, and his own love of order, encouraged him to sort out the vast body of his work. As a student, the author helped him, cataloguing as he titled, numbered and signed the many hundreds of engravings, thus beginning the involvement which has resulted in this book.

Exactly how long he had been suffering from cancer of the throat we do not know but his voice gradually faded to the extent that his speech on leaving the Central in 1979 was almost inaudible. Physically surprisingly strong, he survived a laryngectomy, which removed the problem but left him with only limited means of communication. Few people could understand him, which was frustrating for him and his interlocutors. Especially difficult for him were groups of people with whom he would earlier have had vigorous arguments. By the time he had worked up enough wind to express his point the moment had passed.

His visits to the pub were for the same reason now less frequent and less enjoyable, although he still appreciated his occasional 'peaceful' evenings with Peter Ainger and Joe Lucas, two hard-working local men of natural intelligence and wit. He was perhaps never more relaxed than when listening to their knowledgeable talk of the tides and turns of the river and the hunting of the animals of land, sea and air, punctuated, as it was, by Joe's explanation for almost everything: 'It's Nature, isn't it?'

He died rather suddenly on 6 June 1981, two weeks after a terrible fall sustained while on a visit to his sister Chloris at Wells-next-the-Sea. His ashes were scattered by Peter and Joe, from their duck-punt, on the waters of the River Stour.

NOTES

CHAPTER 1

1. Interview with Rodney Thomas, 1989.

2. BHS himself found her 'wonderful, kind and just' but not 'a warm bosom to cry on'. He later attributed his life-long inability to curb his temper or quell his anger to this lack of soothing maternal warmth. Letter to Anne Ross, 5 October 1951.

3. Scarsdale Lodge in Wright's Lane.

4. Rodney Thomas, who fenced a lot with BHS when they were students, told me how they decided to dress up in the suits of armour that hung around the walls and have a battle. BHS chose a sixteenth-century breast-plate and a curly helmet, 'typical Blair style', while Rodney had chain mail and a 'metal cylinder with holes in it that you put on your shoulders'. When they attacked each other, one with a ball and chain and the other a sword, they were deafened with the noise, and blinded by the rust from the inside of the suits which would earlier have been padded. Realising their mistake they collapsed with laughter and were then unable to get up, wriggling like upturned beetles.

5. Interview with Rodney Thomas, 1989.

6. Interview with Rodney Thomas, 1989.

7. Christopher Neve, *Leon Underwood*, 1974, pp. 86–7.

8. Thomas Balston, 'English Wood-Engraving, 1900–1950', *Image*, No. 5, Autumn 1950, pp. 10–15, and

   See also: John Buckland-Wright, 'The Society of Wood Engravers', *The Studio*, November 1953, pp. 134–41.

   Sarah Hyde, 'British Wood-engraving In the Early Twentieth-Century', *Apollo*, October 1989, pp. 242–47.

9. Christopher Neve, *Leon Underwood*, 1974, p. 72.

10. Interview with Rodney Thomas, 1989.

11. Interview with Rodney Thomas, 1989.

12. Interview with Rodney Thomas, 1989.

CHAPTER 2

1. Jeremy Wilson, *T. E. Lawrence*, 1988, p. 174. Wilson notes that the engraving 'The Poem to S.A.' was not commissioned by Lawrence but that 'four special copies of the subscribers' edition are recorded containing original woodcuts (numbered out of 5)'. At his death the artist left only one copy, numbered 3/8. Eight was also the size of the edition which BHS printed for himself from his other *Seven Pillars* blocks.

2. Lawrence of Arabia, *Seven Pillars of Wisdom*, Penguin, 1962.

3. Jeremy Wilson, *T. E. Lawrence*, 1988, pp. 142–48.

4. T.E.L. letter to Kennington, 1 April 1926, Jeremy Wilson, *T. E. Lawrence*, 1988, p. 171.

5. T.E.L. letter to Manning Pike, 18 October 1926, Jeremy Wilson, *T.E. Lawrence*, 1988, p. 171.

6. Jeremy Wilson, *T.E. Lawrence*, 1988, p. 171.

7. Jeremy Wilson, *T.E. Lawrence*, 1988, p. 175.

8. BHS interview with Paul Collet, 1972.

9. Interview with Rodney Thomas, 1989.

CHAPTER 2 continued

10. *Gertrude Hermes*, Whitechapel Art Gallery, Biographical note, 1967.

11. *The Times* Obituary, 11 May 1983.

12. For the restaurant in the British Pavilion at the World Fair in Paris.

13. (1) The dining room of neighbours Dick and Naomi Mitchison at Rivercourt, Hammersmith. At the break-up of the Hughes-Stanton marriage in 1932 Naomi commissioned Gertrude to replace the unhappy reclining female figure above the sideboard with a flower flanked by a caterpillar and a butterfly — an image of transparent symbolism in the circumstances. (2) The dining room of S. Reckith, 13 Vale, Chelsea.

14. BHS interview with the author, 1979.

15. BHS interview with Paul Collet, 1972.

16. BHS interview with Paul Collet, 1972.

17. John Gould Fletcher, 'Blair Hughes-Stanton', *Print Collectors' Quarterly*, Vol. 21, No. 4, 1934, pp. 360–64.

18. John Gould Fletcher, 'Gertrude Hermes and Blair Hughes-Stanton', *Print Collectors' Quarterly*, Vol. 16, No. 2, 1929, pp. 183–98.

19. Previously published in *Samphire*, Vol. 3, No. 1, p. 22 and p. 24. Published here with the consent of the owner, Ida Graves, and thanks to Laurence Pollinger Ltd and the Estate of Mrs Frieda Lawrence Ravagli.

20. Previously published in *Samphire*, Vol. 3, No. 1, p. 23. Published here with the consent of the owner, Ida Graves, and thanks to Laurence Pollinger Ltd and the Estate of Mrs Frieda Lawrence Ravagli.

21. *D. H. Lawrence, Novelist, Poet, Prophet*, Ed. Stephen Spender, 1973, p. 33.

22. Ida Florence Graves, born 1902, in Mysore, India, daughter of Col. D. H. McD. Graves, Surgeon I.M.S. and of Mabel Alice who came from the Petley family of Naval Commanders. Ida was educated at a Quaker school and at London University.

23. Interview with Rodney Thomas, 1989.

24. Letter to the author from Arthur Calder-Marshall, 1988.

CHAPTER 3

1. James Hamilton, draft MS for 'Gertrude Hermes at Gregynog', *Gertrude Hermes. Selborne*, Gregynog Press, 1988.

2. Dorothy Harrop, *The Gregynog Press*, 1980, p. 72.

3. BHS interview with the author, 1979.

4. James Hamilton, 'Gertrude Hermes at Gregynog', in *Gertrude Hermes. Selborne*, Gregynog Press, 1988.

5. Dorothy Harrop, *The Gregynog Press*, 1980, p. 78.

6. Dorothy Harrop, *The Gregynog Press*, 1980, p. 79.

7. Draft copy of letter from BHS to Miss Davies, 1961.

8. Kathleen Ladizesky, 'Aspects of the Gregynog Press, 1930–33'. *The Private Library*, Third Series, Vol. 7, No. 2, pp. 87–90. Also Kathleen Ladizesky, 'Letters of Stanley Morison to William McCance at Gregynog'. *The Private Library*, Third Series, Vol. 8, No. 3, pp. 124–29.

9. Kathleen Ladizesky, 'Letters of Stanley Morison to William McCance at Gregynog'. *The Private Library*, Third Series, Vol. 8, No. 3, p. 124.

10. Kathleen Ladizesky, 'Letters of Stanley Morison to William McCance at Gregynog'. *The Private Library*, Third Series, Vol. 8, No. 3, p. 123.

11. Kathleen Ladizesky, 'Letters of Stanley Morison to William McCance at Gregynog'. *The Private Library*, Third Series, Vol. 8, No. 3, p. 140.

12. Letter from Gwen Davies to T.J., 18 December 1930, *Thomas Jones C.H. Collection*, Class R, Vol. 3. The National Library of Wales, Aberystwyth.

13. Letter from Gwen Davies to T.J., 16 February 1931, *Thomas Jones C.H. Collection*, Class R, Vol. 3. The National Library of Wales, Aberystwyth.

14. John Gould Fletcher, 'Blair Hughes-Stanton', *Print Collector's Quarterly*, Vol. 21, No. 4, 1934, pp. 364–68.

15. Dorothy Harrop, *The Gregynog Press*, 1980, p. 87.

CHAPTER 3 continued

16. Dorothy Harrop, *The Gregynog Press*, 1980, pp. 87–88.
17. Dorothy Harrop, *The Gregynog Press*, 1980, p. 88.
18. Dorothy Harrop, *The Gregynog Press*, 1980, p. 100.
19. Kathleen Ladizesky, 'Aspects of the Gregynog Press, 1930–33'. *The Private Library*, Third Series, Vol. 7, No. 2, p. 86.
20. *Gertrude Hermes. Selborne*, Gregynog Press, 1988.
21. Kathleen Ladizesky, 'Aspects of the Gregynog Press, 1930–33'. *The Private Library*, Third Series, Vol. 7, No. 2, p. 94.
22. Kathleen Ladizesky, 'Aspects of the Gregynog Press, 1930–33'. *The Private Library*, Third Series, Vol. 7, No. 2, p. 83.
23. Dorothy Harrop, *The Gregynog Press*, 1980, p. 104.
24. Dorothy Harrop, *The Gregynog Press*, 1980, pp. 104–5 and p. 107.
25. Dorothy Harrop, *The Gregynog Press*, 1980, Plate following p. 168.
26. David Chambers, 'Boar's Head and Golden Hours'. *The Private Library*, Third Series, Vol. 8, No. 1, p. 6.
27. David Chambers, 'Boar's Head and Golden Hours'. *The Private Library*, Third Series, Vol. 8, No. 1, p. 26.
28. Kathleen Ladizesky, 'Aspects of the Gregynog Press, 1930–33'. *The Private Library*, Third Series, Vol. 7, No. 2, p. 81.
29. BHS interview with Paul Collet, 1972.
30. Dorothy Harrop, *The Gregynog Press*, 1980, p. 109.
31. Dorothy Harrop, *The Gregynog Press*, 1980, p. 122. Review by Bernard Newdigate in *The London Mercury*, Vol. XXX, September 1934.
32. Dorothy Harrop, *The Gregynog Press*, 1980, p. 115.
33. Dorothy Harrop, *The Gregynog Press*, 1980, p. 106.
34. Kathleen Ladizesky, 'Letters of Stanley Morison to William McCance at Gregynog'. *The Private Library*, Third Series, Vol. 8, No. 3, pp. 140–42, and Dorothy Harrop, *The Gregynog Press*, Private Libraries Association, 1980, p. 98 and p. 100.
35. Letter from Gwen Davies to T.J., 10 May 1932, *Thomas Jones C.H. Collection*, Class R, Vol. 3. National Library of Wales, Aberystwyth.
36. Letter from Gwen Davies to T.J., 1 June 1932, *Thomas Jones C.H. Collection*, Class R, Vol. 3. National Library of Wales, Aberystwyth.
37. Kathleen Ladizesky, 'Letters of Stanley Morison to William McCance at Gregynog'. *The Private Library*, Third Series, Vol. 8, No. 3, pp. 141–42.
38. Letter from William McCance to Gertrude Hermes, 19 June 1932, now in the possession of Gertrude's daughter, Judith Russell.
39. *The Thomas Jones Collection, Diary 1932*, 1 November 1932. National Library of Wales, Aberystwyth.

CHAPTER 4

1. A close friend and admirer of Ida's.
2. Ida has pointed out that at that time she had been separated from her husband, Herbert Marks, for two years.
3. Ida again wished to qualify this account: she had not been influenced by D. H. Lawrence to the extent that BHS had as she had read none of his work except the poems in *Birds, Beasts and Flowers*.
4. BHS interview with the author, 1979.
5. In a letter to the author, 11 February 1989, Ida claimed that she edited and arranged the *Last Poems*: 'Ric. Aldington did the "Introduction" (sic) so one concludes he did the editing . . . But M. Secker got fed up with R.A. doing nothing at all, — so (in Wales) he sent us/me the bundle of typed M.S.S. higgledy-pig, which I achieved happily and easily'.
6. Letter to the author, 1988.
7. D. H. Lawrence, *The Ship of Death and Other Poems*, 1933, p. 28.
8. D. H. Lawrence, *The Ship of Death and Other Poems*, 1933, p. 37.
9. D. H. Lawrence, *The Ship of Death and Other Poems*, 1933, pp. 70–73.

CHAPTER 4 continued

10. Robert Sainsbury was originally a friend of Ida's, and it was she who introduced him to Epstein. BHS introduced him to Henry Moore and to the contemporary art world in general. Sainsbury went on to amass the brilliant collection now housed at the Sainsbury Centre for Visual Art in Norwich. Sir Robert told the author in 1989 that in the early thirties he was a collector of private press books, buying chiefly on the prospectuses. It was because of his liking for books that he was happy to participate in BHS's venture.

11. David Chambers, 'Boar's Head and Golden Hours'. *The Private Library*, Third Series, Vol. 8, No. 1, p. 16.

12. The unbound remainder was published with the Basilisk Press in 1980. Charlene Garry of the Basilisk Press refused to reveal how many were sold and in what form, and the relevant papers appeared to have been destroyed before her death in 1989. A few unbound copies are all that remain to the heirs of BHS's estate.

13. Interview with Ida Graves, 1989.

14. Nos. i, iv, vii, x, xviii and xxi. *Life and Letters*, December 1933–February 1934, pp. 426–30.

15. David Chambers, 'Boar's Head and Golden Hours'. *The Private Library*, Third Series, Vol. 8, No. 1, p. 16.

16. David Chambers, 'Boar's Head and Golden Hours'. *The Private Library*, Third Series, Vol. 8, No. 1, pp. 15–16.

17. Letter to the author, 1988.

18. Taped interview, 1973.

19. John Dreyfus, *A History of the Nonesuch Press*, 1981. Cat. no. 98.

20. Francis Meynell, *My Lives*, 1971, pp. 155–7.

21. Ruari McLean, *Modern Book Design*, 1958.

22. Colin Franklin, *The Private Presses*, Studio Vista, 1969, pp. 138–39.

23. This copy and letter are now in the possession of David Esslemont.

24. *Country Life*, 28 September 1945.

25. Clare Leighton, 'Wood-Engraving of the 1930's', *The Studio*, 1936, pp. 55–6. David Esslemont on this influence: 'I remember BHS looking at one of my prints at the Central [School of Art and Design] and questioning the need for a "mystic floating figure" (*à la BHS*) — it was soon removed!'

26. Letter to the author, 1988.

27. Interview with the late Lady Babette Sainsbury, 1988.

CHAPTER 5

1. BHS interview with the author, 1979.

2. Interview with Ida Graves, 1989.

3. Ministry of Defence War Record.

4. David Fisher, *The War Magician*, Corgi Books, London 1983, p. 22.

5. Ministry of Defence War Record.

6. Edward Howell, *Escape to Live*, Longmans, Green and Co., 1947, p. 33.

7. John Borrie, *Despite Captivity*, William Kimber, 1975, pp. 18–19.

8. Edward Howell, *Escape to Live*, Longmans, Green and Co., 1947, pp. 33–34.

9. John Borrie, *Despite Captivity*, William Kimber, 1975, p. 43.

10. Letters 23 November 1941 to 8 February 1942 to sisters, and to Gertrude who went with her evacuated children to Canada where she worked in the drawing offices of aircraft and shipbuilding factories.

11. Letter to sisters, 24 February 1942.

12. Letter to Gertrude, 20 March 1942.

13. Letter to Gertrude, 28 April 1942.

14. Letter to Gertrude, 11 June 1942.

15. Interview with Ida Graves, 1989.

16. Letter to Gertrude, 29 December 1942.

17. Letter to Gertrude, 4 January 1943.

CHAPTER 5 continued

18. Letter to BHS's daughter Judith, 19 March 1943.
19. Letter to Gertrude, 3 July 1943.

CHAPTER 6

1. Interview with Ida Graves, 1988.
2. BHS interview with the author, 1979.
3. Letter to Anne, 31 December 1951.
4. Letter to Anne, 1 February 1952.
5. Letter to Anne, 26 February 1952.
6. *Art News and Review*, Vol. 6, No. 2, 1954. Ref. David Fraser Jenkins and Sarah Fox-Pitt, *Portrait of the Artist*, The Tate Gallery 1989, p. 52.
7. Letter from Lewis Allen to the author, 25 September 1987.
8. Letter to the author with reference to his commentary in *The Allen Press Bibliography*, 1981, pp. 49–50.
9. Lewis M. Allen, *The Allen Press Bibliography*, 1981, p. 50.
10. Mostly 1958–61.
11. Albert Garrett, *A History of British Wood Engraving*, 1978, p. 291.
12. Lewis M. Allen, *The Allen Press Bibliography*, 1981, pp. 55–56.
13. Letter from Bryan Robertson to BHS, 24 August 1968.
14. Letter from the new director, Mark Glazebrook, 31 July 1969.
15. Roderick Cave, *The Private Press*, 2nd Edition, 1983, p. 267.
16. Letter to the author, 25 September 1987.
17. Letter to the author, 25 September 1987.
18. Interview with the author, 1989.
19. Interview with the author, 1989.
20. Appraisal written for this book, 1989.

ILLUSTRATED BOOKS

1. 1926. SEVEN PILLARS OF WISDOM, By T. E. Lawrence. Pp. xxii + 660. 83–5
$9\frac{7}{8} \times 7\frac{1}{2}$ in. Privately printed. Ten wood-engravings by BHS; some
copies have an extra full-page BHS wood-engraving which illustrates the
dedicatory poem to 'S.A.'. Hand-made paper. 170 complete copies, bound
in full leather, price 30 gns, or given as loose sheets to friends. 32 incomplete copies (lacking some of the plates), half-bound in leather, not for sale
but for distribution to men who had served with Lawrence in Arabia.
*In addition to the engravings by BHS, there were 68 other illustrations, by
various contemporary artists in the text, and there were 61 further illustrations
at the end.*

2. [1927]. ALONE, by Walter de la Mare. Pp. 4. Faber & Gwyer. Coloured
wood-engraving as frontispiece, smaller black and white engraving on
cover. Limited edition: 350 copies on Zanders' hand-made paper,
$7\frac{3}{8} \times 4\frac{5}{8}$ in., with red paper boards, price 5s. Ordinary edition:
$7\frac{1}{4} \times 4\frac{5}{8}$ in., on cream wove paper, in red paper wrappers, price 1s.
Number 4 of the Ariel Poems.

3. 1928. SELF TO SELF. by Walter de la Mare. Faber & Gwyer. One 86
full-page wood-engraving and one smaller one. Limited edition: 500
copies, pp. 14, $8\frac{1}{2} \times 5\frac{3}{8}$ in., on English hand-made paper, in paper
boards, price 5s. Ordinary edition: pp. 4, $7\frac{1}{4} \times 4\frac{3}{4}$ in., on cream wove
paper, in yellow paper wrappers, price 1s.
*Number 11 of the Ariel Poems. Title shown as 'Myself to Myself' on one of the
printer's proofs. The smaller engraving is printed on the cover of the ordinary
edition, on the half-title of the limited edition; the larger engraving serves as a
frontispiece in the ordinary edition, but is printed on the leaf following the title
in the limited edition.*

4. 1928. THE PILGRIM'S PROGRESS, by John Bunyan. Two volumes: 88–9
pp. viii + 175; pp. viii + 163. $14\frac{1}{8} \times 9\frac{3}{4}$ in. Cresset Press. Six full-page
wood-engravings and two smaller ones. Ten copies, on Roman vellum,
bound in niger, price 150 gns. 195 copies, on Batchelor's Kelmscott hand-
made paper, bound in vellum, price $16\frac{1}{2}$ gns.
Four full-page engravings by Gertrude Hermes were also included.

F

87   5. 1929. THE SEARCHER, A War Play (reading version), by Velona Pilcher. Pp. [xiv] + 85. 10 × 7½ in. Heinemann. Nine half-page wood-engravings and a tail-piece. Smooth wove machine-made paper. 1,000 copies for sale in the U.K. First issue, January 1929, quarter bound in maroon clóth, with brick red paper boards, with the tailpiece printed in maroon; brick red dust-jacket, with the tailpiece in maroon; price 10s. 6d. Second issue, May 1930, bound in pale blue cloth, but with the same dust-jacket as the first issue, price 6s. A further 1,000 copies for sale in the U.S.A., published by Doubleday, Doran, New York.

90   6. 1929. THE APOCRYPHA, According to the Authorised Version. Pp. [xii] + 407. 13 × 8¼ in. Cresset Press. One full-page wood-engraving. 30 copies on hand-made paper, with a separate set of the illustrations on Japanese paper, bound in black vellum, in a black cloth-covered double slip-case, price 20 gns. 450 copies on mould-made paper, bound in vellum, in a card slip-case, price 6 gns.
13 engravings by other artists were also included.

91–3   7. 1930. BIRDS, BEASTS AND FLOWERS, by D. H. Lawrence. Pp. viii + 196. 13¼ × 8½ in. The Cresset Press. Ten full-page wood-engravings as chapter headings and frontispiece, two smaller ones as head- and tail-pieces. 30 copies on Batchelor's hand-made paper, of which three, bound in black pigskin, in a black cloth-covered slip-case, were accompanied by a separate set of signed prints, price 30 gns, the others, bound in tan pigskin, in a tan paper-covered slip-case, accompanied by a separate set of unsigned prints, price 3 gns. 500 copies on mould-made paper, quarter bound in vellum, with marbled paper boards, price 3 gns.
The prices given are taken from the prospectus.

94–5   8. 1930. MAYA, by Simon Gantillon. A play paraphrased into English by Virginia and Frank Vernon. Pp. viii + 97. 9¾ × 6½ in. Golden Cockerel Press. Six full-page and seven smaller wood-engravings. Van Gelder hand-made paper. 500 copies, bound in maize buckram. Price 35s.

t-p, 96–7   9. 1931. THE LOVERS' SONG BOOK, by W. H. Davies. Pp. vi + 30. 8¾ × 6 in. Printed at the Gregynog Press, but not published. 64 wood-engravings: one full-page engraving of Cupid as frontispiece; 3 smaller ones on title and contents pages; engraved initials and tailpieces to each of the 30 poems. Japanese vellum, with the engravings in sepia. According to BHS about twelve copies were printed, including two on vellum. Three of those on Japanese vellum were bound in 1975/6 by Paul Collet in quarter niger with hand-made paper boards, in slip-cases.

10. 1931. COMUS, A mask, by John Milton. Pp. [x] + 28. 11 × 6¾ in.   98–103
Gregynog Press. Six full-page wood-engravings, and two smaller ones on
title-page and as tail-piece. Japanese vellum. 25 copies bound by George
Fisher to a design by BHS, of unpolished dun-coloured levant morocco
decorated with blind and gilt embossed lines and a blind title panel, price
138s. 225 copies quarter bound in buckram, with buff paper boards, price
35s.

11. 1932. CANIADAU, gan W. J. Gruffydd. Pp. viii + 103. 10⅛ × 7⅛ in.   104–5
Gregynog Press. Four wood-engravings, and shadow initial letters.
Barcham Green Charles I grey hand-made paper. 25 copies bound by
George Fisher to a design by BHS, of polished brown levant morocco,
decorated with vertical gilt lines and raised bands outlined in blind, price
6 gns. 275 copies quarter bound in grey cloth, with Tyrian red paper
boards. Price 1 gn.

12. 1932. THE TRAGICALL HISTORY OF DOCTOR FAUSTUS, As it hath been   106–9
acted by the Right Honorable the Earle of Nottingham his servants, by
Christopher Marlowe. Pp. viii + 57. 10¾ × 7⅞ in. Golden Hours Press.
Four full-page wood-engravings and one half-page. Millbourn hand-made
paper. 250 copies: about 40 quarter bound in red morocco, with marbled
boards, in slip-case, price 2½ gns; the remainder taken over by Hollis &
Carter, bound in green buckram, in slip-case.

13. 1932 [1933]. EREWHON, by Samuel Butler. Pp. [ii] + 268. 9⅛ × 6 in.   110–13
Gregynog Press. 29 wood-engraved head-pieces. Japanese vellum. 25
copies bound by George Fisher to a design by BHS, of polished brown
levant morocco, decorated with bands of parallel horizontal gilt-tooled
lines joined or terminated on back and front covers with semicircular lines;
gilt titling and imprint are incorporated on the spine and cover as well as
the (completion) date, 1932, at the base of the four-ribbed spine; price
8 gns. 275 copies bound in sage green Welsh sheepskin, price 3 gns.

14. 1933. THE REVELATION OF SAINT JOHN THE DIVINE. Pp. [60].   114–21
13⅝ × 8 in. Gregynog Press. 41 wood-engravings: 13 full-page, 15 smaller,
13 with lettering, and title-page lettering and press device. Japanese
vellum. 18 copies bound by George Fisher to a design by BHS, of
unpolished cream levant morocco, with a crushed panel incorporating a
cross of black onlaid calf with gilt-tooled shading, the words THE
REVELATION in gilt, and a rectangle of onlaid brown calf with the rest of the
title and tooling in blind; a similar, smaller design on the back bears the
imprint; the spine is ribbed with the title and GG in gilt; price 12 gns. 232
copies in red Hermitage calf with title and press device by BHS blocked in
blind on the front, price 6 gns.

122   15. 1933. ABOUT LEVY, by Arthur Calder-Marshall. Pp. 252. 7½ × 5 in. Jonathan Cape. Frontispiece wood-engraving and small one on title-page. Cream wove machine-made paper. Bound in black cloth. Dust-jacket repeating both engravings. Price 7s. 6d.

vi, 123–7   16. 1933. FOUR POEMS ('L'Allegro', 'Il Penseroso', 'Arcades' and 'Lycidas'), by John Milton. Pp. 35. 10⅛ × 6½ in. Gregynog Press. Four full-page wood-engravings, and seven smaller ones used for title and tail-pieces. Japanese vellum. 14 copies bound by George Fisher to a design by BHS, of unpolished dun coloured levant morocco, decorated on both covers with gilt-outlined crushed panels filled with lines tooled in blind; the five-ribbed spine bears similar panels and the titling and imprint in blind; price 7 gns. One copy bound by George Fisher, to his own design, in polished levant morocco, price 7 gns. 235 copies in red Herimitage calf with a design derived from the frontispiece engraving blocked in blind on the front, price 2 gns.

133–7   17. 1933. THE SHIP OF DEATH AND OTHER POEMS, by D. H. Lawrence. Pp. x + 106. 10 × 6¼ in. Martin Secker. Ten full-page wood-engravings and three smaller ones. Basingwerk Parchment. 1,500 copies, quarter bound in black cloth, with pale brick red hand-made paper boards. Dust-jacket. Price 10s 6d.

138   18. 1934. TO-MORROW IS A NEW DAY, A fantasy, by T. O'B. Hubbard. Pp. vi + 125. 10 × 6¼ in. Lincoln Williams. Eight full-page wood-engravings. Basingwerk Parchment. Quarter bound in green cloth with black paper boards. Price 1 gn.

139   19. 1934. ELEGIES AND SONGS, by John Mavrogordato. Pp. 30 (including front cover). 8½ × 5½ in. Cobden-Sanderson. One wood-engraving on the cover. Basingwerk Parchment paper. Paper covers. Price 2s.

140–1   20. 1934. PRIMEVAL GODS, by Christopher Sandford. Pp. 30. 9 × 5½ in. Boar's Head Press. Eight small wood-engravings: a floral design for the title-page and a head-piece for each of the seven poems. Joynson mould-made paper. 25 copies quarter bound in vellum, with pale green cloth boards, with a separate set of the engravings on Japanese vellum, price 1 gn. 125 copies bound in pale green cloth, price 10s. 6d.

128–32   21. 1933 [1934]. THE LAMENTATIONS OF JEREMIAH. Pp. [30]. 15⅛ × 10 in. Gregynog Press. Five full-page wood-engravings as chapter openings, 16 smaller ones, initial lettering and title-page. Japanese vellum. 15 copies bound by George Fisher to a design by BHS, of unpolished black levant morocco, decorated with a complex design on both covers of an onlaid circle of blue Oasis morocco, six onlaid white squares of increasing size, parallel lines tooled in gilt and blind and a sword, half in gilt and half in blind; the spine has six raised bands outlined in blind with the sword, titling, device and date tooled in gilt; price 12 gns. 125 copies bound in dark blue Hermitage calf, and 110 in dark blue Oasis morocco, slip-case, price 5 gns.

22. 1934. ECCLESIASTES, OR THE PREACHER. Pp. 23. 13 × 9¼ in. Golden   143–5
Cockerel Press. 13 wood-engravings of varying height, but all six inches
wide, the width of the text. 3 copies on vellum, bound in white pigskin,
price 30 gns. 247 copies, on Batchelor's hand-made paper, quarter bound
in vellum, with orange cloth boards, price 3 gns.

23. 1934. A CRIME AGAINST CANIA, by Arthur Calder-Marshall.   146–7
Pp. [ii] + 67. 9½ × 6¼ in. Golden Cockerel Press. Four half-page wood-
engravings. Batchelor hand-made paper. 250 copies, quarter bound in
black morocco, with decorated cloth boards. Price 1 gn.

24. 1934. THE DEVIL AND ALL, Six short stories, by John Collier.   142
Pp. iii + 125. 9 × 5½ in. Nonesuch Press and (in U.S.A.) Random House.
One full-page wood-engraving as frontispiece. Japanese vellum. 1,000
copies bound in green cloth. Dust-jacket. Price 12s. 6d.

25. 1934 [1935]. EPITHALAMION, A Poem by Ida Graves with Associate   148–53
Wood-engraving by Blair Hughes-Stanton. Pp. [51] (unnumbered).
13½ × 8 in. Gemini Press. 23 full-page wood-engravings, each facing a
stanza. Printed by BHS. 50 copies printed on Japanese vellum; 280 copies
on Basingwerk Parchment.
About 25 copies on Japanese vellum, quarter bound by Sangorski &
Sutcliffe in the 1930s to a design by BHS, in French levant morocco with
rose coloured Winterstroke Tudor Brick hand-made paper boards, price
5 gns. 6 copies on Japanese vellum, bound in 1980 to a new design by BHS
of dark blue morocco decorated with gold tooling and inlays of black and
white, with extra pages on the history of the book and a list of books with
engravings by BHS, sold by the Basilisk Press, price £800–£1,000.
About 125 copies on Basingwerk Parchment, bound in the 1930s in pale
green Ingres paper boards, price 30s. For the remaining copies Basilisk
offered a choice of a binding in the rose coloured paper of the original
edition edged with dark brown leather, price £175–£200, or the loose
sheets, folded but not stitched, in a folder and slip-case covered in the pale
green Ingres paper of the original edition, price £110–£180.
Some unbound copies remain, but the destruction of the relevant file by
Charlene Garry during her last illness has made it impossible to know how
many copies were sold and in what form.

26. 1935. AN APPROACH TO ART, A pictorial guide to twelve broadcast talks
and discussions on The Artist and his Public, by Eric Newton. Pp. viii + 32
plates. 9¾ × 7¼ in. B.B.C. Full-page wood-engraving on cover,
'designed for this pamphlet' by BHS. Card covers. Price 7d.

154–5   27. 1935. PASTORAL, OR VIRTUE REQUITED, by H.H.M. [Herbert H. Marks]. Pp. 39. $9 \times 5\frac{5}{8}$ in. Gemini Press. Four full-page wood-engravings. Printed by BHS. Pannekoek mould-make paper. 120 copies quarter bound in tan coloured buckram with sage green paper boards. Price 15s.

156   28. 1936. THE NATIONAL MARK CALENDAR OF COOKING, compiled for The Ministry of Agriculture by Ambrose Heath and D. D. Cottington Taylor. Pp. 128. $7\frac{1}{4} \times 4\frac{3}{4}$ in. Ministry of Agriculture and Fisheries. Twelve small wood-engravings as head-pieces to each month's recipes. January 1936, 100,000 copies (printed by 'CT&CoLtd'); April 1936, 200,000 copies (printed by 'P&SLtd'). Light grey-green card covers.

29. 1936. ADDRESS BY ABRAHAM LINCOLN AT THE DEDICATION OF THE NATIONAL CEMETERY AT GETTYSBURG. Pp. [4]. $10\frac{1}{2} \times 6\frac{3}{4}$ in. Privately printed by BHS at the Gemini Press for Robert Sainsbury. Unillustrated. Imperial Japanese vellum. 50 copies bound in dark green morocco. Not for sale.

157   30. 1940. GWELEDIGAETHEU Y BARDD CWSC, Visions of the Sleeping Bard, by Ellis Wynne, translated by T. Gwynn Jones. Pp. xii + 216. $10\frac{7}{8} \times 7\frac{7}{8}$ in. Gregynog Press. One full-page wood-engraving as frontispiece. Barcham Green hand-made paper. 20 copies bound to his own design by George Fisher, in polished purple Oasis morocco, price 9 gns. 155 copies quarter bound in red Oasis morocco, with plum coloured cloth boards, price 25s.

158   31. [1942]. MOTHER AND CHILD, A poem by Ida Graves. Pp. 24. $7\frac{3}{8} \times 5$ in. Fortune Press. One full-page wood-engraving (1934 Christmas card entitled 'Charity') as frontispiece, a very small one on the half-title and another as tail-piece (both from *The Lovers' Song Book*, 1931). Adelphi cream laid machine-made paper. Bound in red buckram. Dust-jacket. Price 5s.

32. 1945. VOICES ON THE GREEN, edited by A. R. J. Wise and Reginald A. Smith. Pp. 224. $7\frac{1}{4} \times 4\frac{3}{4}$ in. Michael Joseph. One full-page wood-engraving as frontispiece, reproduced by permission of the B.B.C. Machine-made paper. Bound in blue cloth. Dust-jacket. Price 10s. 6d.
The engraving used was 'Joy Bells', reduced from a Christmas card commissioned by the B.B.C. in 1933. Engravings by other artists were also included.

159   33. 1946. AFRICAN FOLK TALES, by Yoti Lane. Pp. 240. $7\frac{1}{4} \times 4\frac{3}{4}$ in. Peter Lunn. Ten full-page scraperboard drawings on coloured grounds, and seven smaller ones used as chapter headings. Two of the latter reduced and adapted for the title and contents pages; one of the full-page drawings repeated as a frontispiece and part of another on the dust-jacket. Cream wove machine-made paper. Bound in buff cloth. Price 8s. 6d.

34. 1948. THE CONFESSIONS OF AN ENGLISH OPIUM-EATER, by Thomas de Quincey. Pp. xiv + 219. 8½ × 5 in. Folio Society. Ten half-page wood-engravings. Machine-made Antique laid paper. First impression, 3,529 copies. Bound in black cloth. Dust-jacket with the sixth engraving repeated on the front. Price 16s.

159–60

1963. Second edition, reset. Pp. xvi + 230. 8½ × 5½ in. Machine-made smooth wove paper. First impression, 4,000 copies. Bound in black cloth. Slip-case. Price 23s. 6d.

The engravings had been cut in 1930 for the Fanfrolico Press, which went bankrupt before publication. A very much better impression was obtained on the smoother paper used for the second edition.

35. 1949. SENSE AND SENSIBILITY, by Jane Austen. Pp. 302 + 8 plates. 8½ × 5½ in. Avalon Press. Eight full-page colour drawings (reproduced by photo-litho), and 21 black and white drawings as chapter-headings. Cream wove machine-made paper. Bound in green buckram. Price 15s. *Castell Polychrome pencils were used for the colour drawings, Conté Pencil for the others.*

36. 1950. THE EUSTACE DIAMONDS, by Anthony Trollope. Two volumes: pp. xvi + 362 + 8 plates; pp. viii + 384 + 8 plates. 8 × 5 in. Oxford University Press. 16 full-page drawings (reproduced by photo-litho), and 15 smaller ones in the text. Cream wove machine-made paper. Bound in brown cloth. Dust-jacket with one of the drawings on the front. Slip-case. Price 30s.

1973. Second impression, as O.U.P. paperback. Pp. xvi + 746. 7⅜ × 4¾ in. Reprinted lithographically from the earlier edition, but omitting the full-page plates. White wove machine-made paper. Black paper covers, with scraperboard illustration on the front. Price 75p.

1983. World's Classics. Pp. xliv + 364 + 414. 7¼ × 4½ in. Paperback.

37. 1951. A ZOO IN YOUR HOUSE, A selection of animal stories compiled and with an introduction by Hugh Anderson. Pp. 221. 8½ × 5½ in. Dennis Yates. Five full-page scraperboard drawings, one repeated as frontispiece, and 11 small ones as head-pieces. Cream wove machine-made paper. Bound in red cloth. Dust-jacket.

38. 1956. THE WRECK OF THE GOLDEN MARY, A saga of the California Gold Rush, by Charles Dickens and Wilkie Collins. Pp. 90. 10⅜ × 7 in. Allen Press. Seven large wood-engravings as head-pieces. Japanese vellum. 200 copies quarter bound in pale brick red paper, with grey marbled paper boards. Price $15.00. 15 sets of the engravings, in a portfolio, price $7.50.

161–3

39. 1959. YOUTH, by Joseph Conrad. Pp. [57]. 15½ × 10¼ in. Allen Press. Eight nine-colour linocuts, the width of the text but of varying height. Richard de Bas hand-made paper. 140 copies bound in white parchment paper, with part of one of the linocuts on the front. Blue, Japanese paper-covered slip-case. Price $35.00.
Progresively cut, elimination linocuts were printed from line-blocks made from stage-proofs provided by BHS.

40. 1966. MORE PAPERS HAND MADE BY JOHN MASON, by John Mason. 5 leaves, printed on rectos only + 35 specimens of 12 × 8 papers, interleaved with sheets of Tuckenhay hand-made paper. One coloured linocut (made for the book and printed by BHS), and two full-page wood-engravings, from *The Ship of Death*. 140 copies: bound in Linson Vellum, price 25 gns; or with up to five extra specimens, bound in Linson Vellum or leather, usually 35 gns.

41. 1961. THE SCARLET BOY, by Arthur Calder Marshall. Pp. 222. 7¾ × 5 in. Rupert Hart-Davis. Bound in red cloth. Dust-jacket design by BHS. Price 16s.
The dust-jacket is decorated on the front cover and spine with a linocut in red, blue, black and grey, incorporating the titling engraved in white line though the black.

164   42. 1963. THE BEAST IN THE JUNGLE, A psychological novel, by Henry James. Pp. [93]. 15 × 10 in. Allen Press. 16 wood-engravings overprinted with linocut patterns: one full-page as frontispiece, six half-page, and nine quarter-page. Arches mould-made paper. 130 copies, bound in Italian hand-made paper boards. Acetate dust-jacket. Price $38.50. 15 sets of artist's proofs, printed by BHS, in a portfolio, price $160.00.

165   43. 1970. THE BOOK OF GENESIS, Pp. [112]. 12¾ × 9¼ in. Allen Press. 24 full-page linocuts, reduced. 140 copies. Umbria hand-made paper. Bound in green cloth boards. Price $100.00. 10 sets of artist's proofs (full size), printed by BHS, 8 sets for sale, in a portfolio, price $500.00.

44. 1973. FOUR FICTIONS, 'The Lagoon' by Joseph Conrad, 'The Legend of Saint Julian' by Gustave Flaubert, 'The Jolly Corner' by Henry James, and 'The Annuity' by Luigi Pirandello. Pp. 155. 14¼ × 9¾ in. Allen Press. Each story printed in a different face on different paper: Conrad, with a full-page, three-colour linocut (reduced) by BHS, and, as tail-piece, the cover-device from *Youth*; printed on Wookey Hole hand-made paper. Charter Oak hand-made paper boards. Acetate dust-jacket. Price $100.00.

INDEPENDENT ENGRAVINGS

1924.	Bathers	$7 \times 9\frac{3}{8}$	A few hand-prints only.	
1924.	The Song	$9\frac{3}{8} \times 7$	A few hand-prints only.	
1924.	Problem M	7×5	A few hand-prints only.	166
1925.	Sunbathers	4×5	A few hand-prints only.	
1925.	3me Classe	$4\frac{1}{2} \times 3\frac{3}{4}$	A few hand-prints only.	8
1925.	The Hero	7×5	A few hand-prints only.	
1925.	Quoits	$6\frac{1}{2} \times 5$	A few hand-prints only.	167
1925.	Italian Washhouse	5×7	30	
1925/6.	Peasant Family and Babe/Midday Rest	$2\frac{3}{4} \times 5\frac{1}{2}$	30	
1925/6.	Playtime	$2\frac{3}{4} \times 5\frac{1}{2}$	30	
1926.	Proud Parents	$2\frac{3}{4} \times 5\frac{1}{2}$	30	168
1926.	Lovers	$2\frac{3}{4} \times 5\frac{1}{2}$	30	168
1926.	The Model	$6\frac{1}{2} \times 4$	A few hand-prints only.	169
1926.	Siesta	$4\frac{1}{4} \times 6\frac{1}{4}$	30	
1926.	The Fugitive	$3\frac{3}{4} \times 2\frac{3}{4}$	30	
1927.	The Boat	5×7	30	
1927.	Negroid/Black Bottom	$6\frac{3}{4} \times 4\frac{3}{4}$	30	
1927.	6 a.m.	$5\frac{1}{2} \times 4\frac{1}{8}$	A few hand-prints only.	
1929.	Emancipation of Woman	$7\frac{1}{8} \times 4$	30	171
1929.	The Maze	$5\frac{5}{8} \times 4\frac{3}{4}$	30	170
1929.	The Vortex	7×5	30	
1929.	Nude	$3\frac{7}{8} \times 7\frac{1}{8}$	30	
1929.	Turkish Bath	7×9	30	14
1930.	Rebirth	12×8	30	20
1930.	A Man Died	12×8	30	18
1934.	The Shore	9×13	20	Colour on pearwood.	
1935.	The Rock	14×9	20	Colour on pearwood.	
1935.	Horizon	$13 \times 9\frac{1}{2}$	20	Colour on pearwood.	
1935.	Composition	$9\frac{1}{2} \times 14\frac{1}{2}$	25	Colour on pearwood.	
1935.	Holy Family/Composition	$6\frac{5}{8} \times 11$	15		172
1936.	Creation/Composition	$8 \times 12\frac{1}{8}$	20		173
1937.	Two Figures I	$9 \times 11\frac{1}{2}$	15		174
1937.	Figures II	$9\frac{1}{8} \times 11\frac{1}{2}$	15		175
1938.	Two Figures Vertical/ Composition	$15\frac{5}{8} \times 10\frac{3}{4}$	17		46

177	1938.	Conversation	4 × 6	20	
176	1938.	Venus/Nude	4½ × 7½	20	
	1950.	Leda and Swan	9 × 12½	30	Pearwood & lino.
	1950.	Europa and the Bull	8 × 6	43	Pearwood & lino.
	1950.	Fleur du Mal	6⅛ × 4	45	Pearwood & lino.
	1951.	Night	9¼ × 12⅞	30	Pearwood & lino.
			+ 2nd edn	XXXVI	

The following were all colour linocuts

1950.	Bathers/The Intruder	10 × 13½	24
1951.	Odysseus, Scylla and		
	Charybdis	15¾ × 10	30
1951.	Dawn	17 × 20	40
1958.	Sun down, Sun up	13¾ × 19½	30
1958.	Evening	12½ × 24	30
1958.	Estuary	6 × 27¾	34
1958.	Pursuit	7½ × 29¾	30
1958.	Pursuit Vertical	26 × 7½	30
1958.	Midsummer Night	18 × 30	36
1959.	Rock Pool	12 × 20¼	38
1959.	Matrix	13½ × 19½	40
1959.	Summer Storm	19½ × 10¼	40
1959.	Thunderstorm	13⅜ × 19¾	40
1960.	Eclipse	12 × 20¼	39
1960.	Moonshine	28½ × 19	35
1960.	The Rock	28½ × 17¾	40
1960.	The Wave	19 × 28½	36
1961.	The Cove	28½ × 17¾	36

Engraved Bookplates

	Basil Burton	4 × 2¾
	Christopher and Catherine Eastwood	3½ × 2½
1953.	Marc and Ismini Fitch	4 × 3

SELECT BIBLIOGRAPHY

Allen, Lewis M. *The Allen Press Bibliography*, The Allen Press, California, 1981.

Balston, Thomas. 'English Wood-Engraving 1900–1950', *Image*: 5 (Autumn 1950), pp. 1–84.

Bliss, Douglas Percy. *A History of Wood-Engraving*, Dent, 1928.

Buckland-Wright, John. 'The Society of Wood-Engravers', *The Studio*, Vol. 146, No. 728 (1953), pp. 134–41.

Cave, Roderick. *The Private Press*, Faber, 1971. 2nd edition: R. R. Bowker, 1983.

Chambers, David. 'Boar's Head and Golden Hours', *The Private Library*, Third Series, Vol. 8, No. 1 (Spring 1985), pp. 3–34.

Collet, Paul. *Blair Hughes-Stanton*, Thesis for Camberwell School of Arts and Crafts, 1972.

Dreyfus, John. *A History of the Nonesuch Press*, Nonesuch Press, 1981.

Duval, Elizabeth. *T. E. Lawrence, A Bibliography*, Arrow Editions, New York, 1938.

Finberg, Alexander J. 'The Recent Work of Mr Hughes-Stanton, ARA', *The Studio*, Vol. 75, No. 307 (Autumn 1918), pp. 3–10.

Fletcher, John Gould. 'Gertrude Hermes and Blair Hughes-Stanton', *Print Collector's Quarterly*, Vol. XVI (1929), pp. 183–98.

Fletcher, John Gould. 'Blair Hughes-Stanton', *Print Collector's Quarterly*, Vol. XXI (1934), pp. 353–72.

Garret, Albert. *A History of British Wood Engraving*, Midas Books, Tunbridge Wells, 1978.

German-Reed, T. *Bibliographical Notes on T. E. Lawrence's "Seven Pillars of Wisdom" and "Revolt in the Desert"*, W. & G. Foyle, 1928.

Godfrey, Richard. *Printmaking in Britain*, Phaidon, 1978.

Graves, Affleck. *Elarna Cane*, Faber, 1956.

Hamilton, James. 'Gertrude Hermes at Gregynog', *Gertrude Hermes. Selbourne*, Gregynog Press, 1988.

Franklin, Colin. *The Private Presses*, Studio Vista, 1969.

Harrop, Dorothy. *The Gregynog Press*, Private Libraries Association, 1980.

Hutchins, Michael. *Printing at Gregynog: Aspects of a Great Private Press*, Welsh Arts Council, 1976.

Jones, Thomas. *The Gregynog Press: A Paper Read to the Double Crown Club on 7 April 1954*, Oxford University Press, 1954.

Ladizesky, Kathleen. 'Aspects of the Gregynog Press, 1930–33', *The Private Library*, Third Series, Vol. 7, No. 2 (Summer 1984), pp. 79–98.

Ladizesky, Kathleen. 'Letters of Stanley Morison to William McCance at Gregynog', *The Private Library*, Third Series, Vol. 8, No. 3 (Autumn 1985), pp. 117–43.

Leighton, Clare. *Wood-Engraving and Woodcuts*, The Studio, 1932.

Leighton, Clare. *Wood-Engraving of the 1930's*, The Studio, 1936.

Lewis, John. 'The Wood-Engravings of Blair Hughes-Stanton', *Image*: 6 (Spring 1951), pp. 26–44.

Mackley, George. *Wood Engraving*, National Magazine Co., 1948. Republished: Gresham Books, 1985.

McLean Ruari. *Modern Book Design*, Faber, 1958.

Meynell, Francis. *My Lives*, Bodley Head, 1971.

Neve, Christopher. *Leon Underwood*, Thames and Hudson, 1974.

Newdigate, Bernard. *The Art of the Book*, The Studio, 1938.

O'Brien, Philip M. *T. E. Lawrence: A Bibliography*, St Paul's Bibliographies, 1988.

Sandford, Christopher. 'The Wood-Engraved Illustration', *The Studio*, Vol. 139, No. 683 (1950), pp. 50–55.

Spender, Stephen (Ed.) et al. *D. H. Lawrence: Novelist, Poet, Prophet*, Weidenfeld and Nicolson, 1973.

Whitechapel Art Gallery. *Gertrude Hermes*, London, 1967.

Wilson, Jeremy. *T. E. Lawrence*, National Portrait Gallery Publications, 1988.

Wilson, Jeremy. *Lawrence of Arabia*, Heinemann, 1989.

THE ENGRAVINGS

SEVEN PILLARS OF WISDOM, 1926   83
'The Poem to S.A.'

SEVEN PILLARS OF WISDOM, 1926
'The Sport of Kings'; 'Standards of Value'

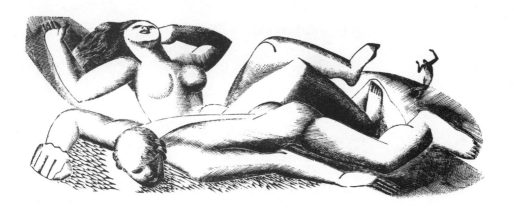

SEVEN PILLARS OF WISDOM, 1926   85
'Conscience Our Guide'; 'The Body Survives the Soul'

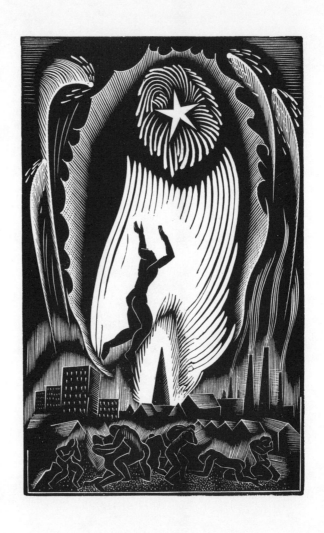

SELF TO SELF, 1928

THE SEARCHER, 1929 THEATRE ARTS MONTHLY, 1926 87
Scene Three   'The Bull and the Beast'

THE PILGRIM'S PROGRESS, 1928
'The River of Death' (reduced from 9¾ × 7 in)

THE PILGRIM'S PROGRESS, 1928   89
'Christiana Joins Christian' (reduced from 9⅜ × 6⅞ in)

THE APOCRYPHA, 1929
'Susannah'

BIRDS, BEASTS AND FLOWERS, 1930   91
'The Beginning'; 'The End'

92   BIRDS, BEASTS AND FLOWERS, 1930
                                             'Flowers'

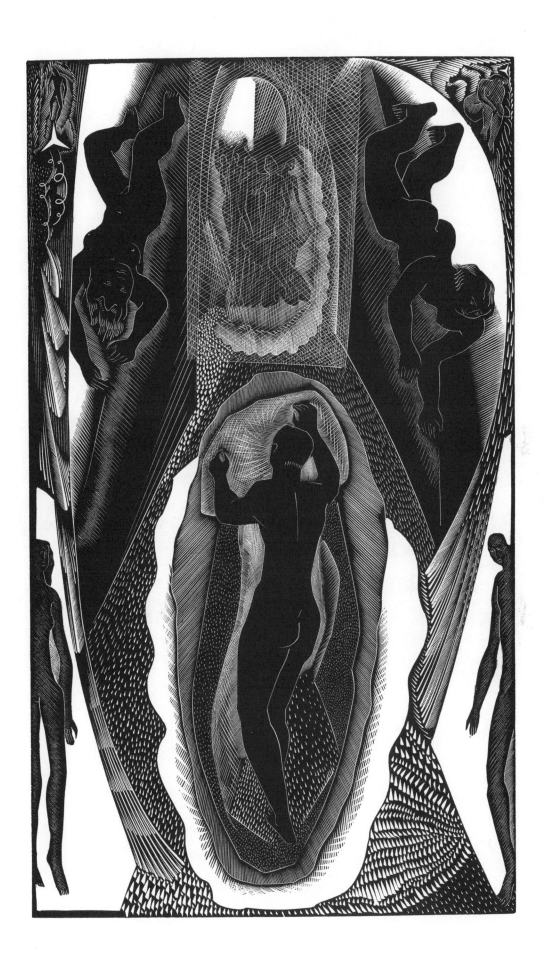

BIRDS, BEASTS AND FLOWERS, 1930   93
'Ghosts'

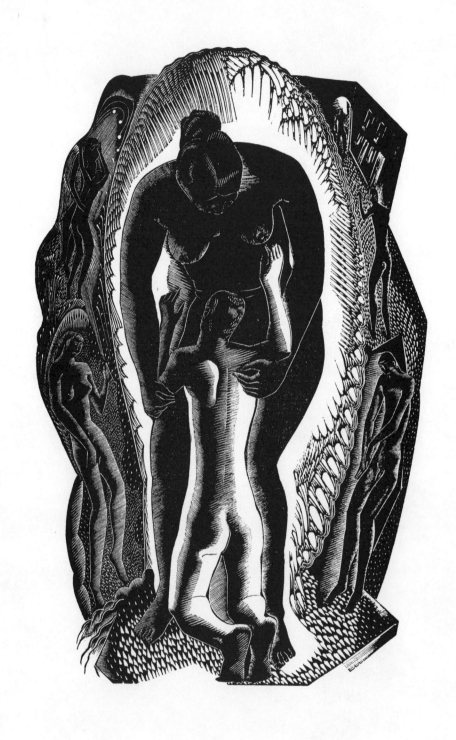

94   MAYA, 1930

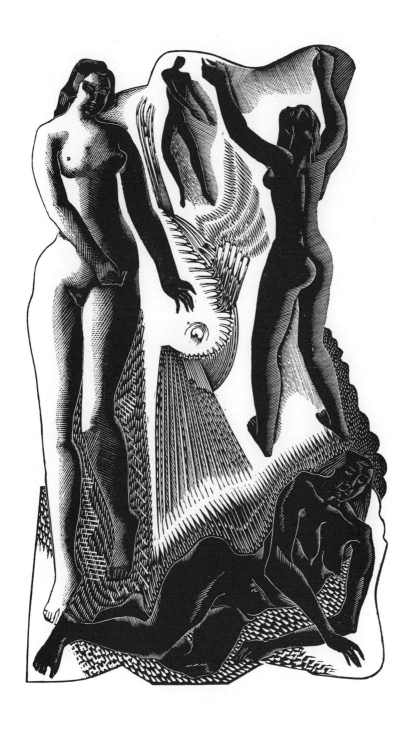

MAYA, 1930   95

THIS OLD GREEN ORCHARD

THE healthiest place for Love is here,
    And not in any room;
Out in this old, green orchard,
    With the apple-trees in bloom.

For here we see no idle hooks,
    No empty shelf or box,
To set Love's thoughts on sable scarves,
    Or stoles of silver fox.

The first sweet lovers known to life
    Had nothing more than this:
Shall we, far richer when compared,
    Be poorer in our bliss?

16

PECKING

ONE kiss to open up the day,
   One kiss at night, to close it fast;
Sometimes a kiss or two between,
   To help the first and last.
But when I woke this morning
   ~~~~~~~~~~ early,
I caught her pecking at my face;
Greedy for grain, she pecked and
   ~~~~~~~ pecked,
   All over the golden place.
And artful I, still feigning sleep,
Lay quiet, while that little chick
Enjoyed the grain Love scattered
   ~~~~~~~~~ there,
   And still went on to peck.

17
f

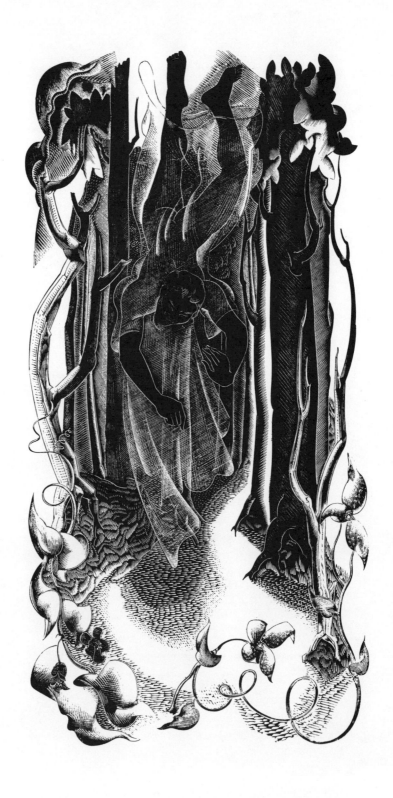

98

COMUS, 1931
'The Brothers'

100   COMUS, 1931
                                 'The Attendant Spirit'

COMUS, 1931
'The Lady'

101

H

102

COMUS, 1931
'Comus'

103

106   THE TRAGICALL HISTORY OF DOCTOR FAUSTUS, 1932
'Helen'

THE TRAGICALL HISTORY OF DOCTOR FAUSTUS, 1932　　107
'Good and Evil Angels'

108   THE TRAGICALL HISTORY OF DOCTOR FAUSTUS, 1932
'Faustus Descends into Hell'

THE TRAGICALL HISTORY OF DOCTOR FAUSTUS, 1932   109
'Mephistopheles'

EREWHON, 1932 [1933]
'Fond Parents'; 'The Birth Formula'

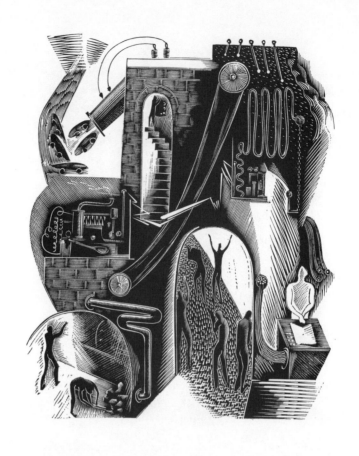

EREWHON, 1932 [1933]
'Machine Age'; 'Machine Revolt'

EREWHON, 1932 [1933]   113
'In the Wood Shed'; 'The World of the Unborn'

THE REVELATION OF SAINT JOHN THE DIVINE, 1933
'The Whore of Babylon'

THE REVELATION OF SAINT JOHN THE DIVINE, 1933   115
'The Mighty Angel'

116   THE REVELATION OF SAINT JOHN THE DIVINE, 1933
'There Was a Wonder in Heaven'

THE REVELATION OF SAINT JOHN THE DIVINE, 1933   117
'The War'

I

118   THE REVELATION OF SAINT JOHN THE DIVINE, 1933
'The Moon'; 'The Sun'; 'The Woman'

THE REVELATION OF SAINT JOHN THE DIVINE, 1933   119
'The White Horse'

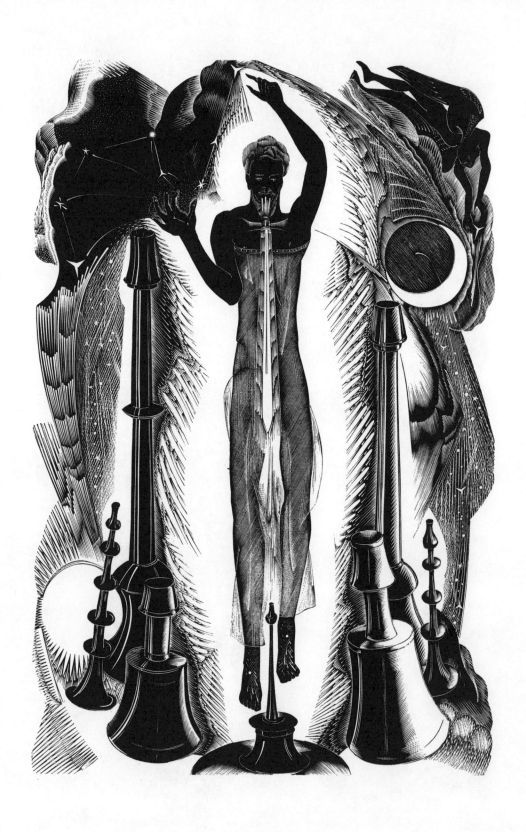

THE REVELATION OF SAINT JOHN THE DIVINE, 1933
'Son of Man'

THE REVELATION OF SAINT JOHN THE DIVINE, 1933 121
'Apollyon'

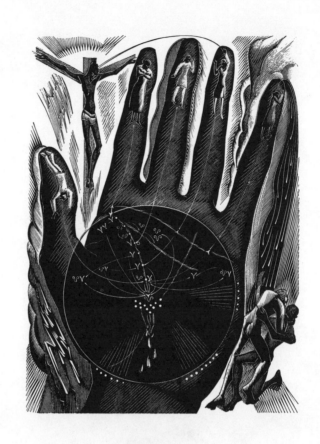

ABOUT LEVY, 1933
'Controls'; title-page device

124

FOUR POEMS, 1933
'Daphnis with Aurora'

126

FOUR POEMS, 1933
'Arcades'

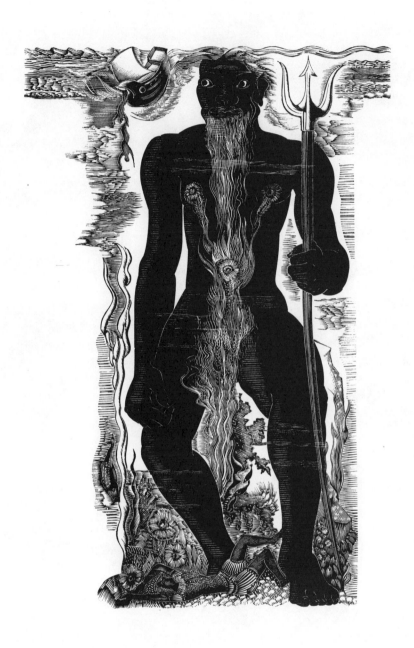

FOUR POEMS, 1933   127
'Neptune'

THE LAMENTATIONS OF JEREMIAH, 1933 (1934)
'The City Mourns II'; 'Daughter of Edom II'

THE LAMENTATIONS OF JEREMIAH, 1933 (1934) 129
'The Man Mourns I'; 'Daughter of Edom I'

130   THE LAMENTATIONS OF JEREMIAH, 1933 (1934)
'The City'

THE LAMENTATIONS OF JEREMIAH, 1933 (1934)   131
'The Man'

132   THE LAMENTATIONS OF JEREMIAH, 1933 (1934)
'Sons and Daughters'

THE SHIP OF DEATH AND OTHER POEMS, 1933   133
'The Ship'; 'Beyond'

THE SHIP OF DEATH AND OTHER POEMS, 1933
'Gentian'

THE SHIP OF DEATH AND OTHER POEMS, 1933   135
'Whales'

136   THE SHIP OF DEATH AND OTHER POEMS, 1933
'The Triumph'

THE SHIP OF DEATH AND OTHER POEMS, 1933   137
'The Cross'

TOMORROW IS A NEW DAY, 1934
'The Evangelist'

PRIMEVAL GODS, 1934
'Spring Song'; 'The Maiden'

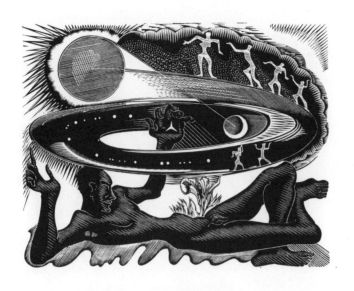

PRIMEVAL GODS, 1934   141
'Eternity'; 'Alone'

THE DEVIL AND ALL, 1934
Frontispiece

ECCLESIASTES, 1934
'All is Vanity'

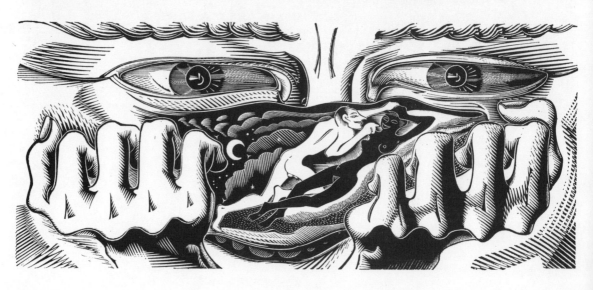

ECCLESIASTES, 1934
'Enjoy Pleasure'; 'To Everything There is a Season'; 'The Creator'

ECCLESIASTES, 1934   145
'The Preacher'; 'The Offering'; 'I Have Seen'; 'The Sower'

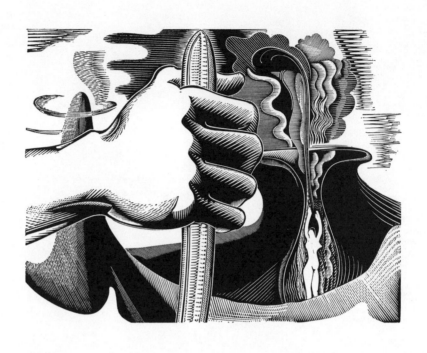

146 1 46

A CRIME AGAINST CANIA, 1934
'Crater'; 'Mother Cania'

A CRIME AGAINST CANIA, 1934   147
'Supplication'; 'A Dream'

148   EPITHALAMION, 1934 [1935]
                                                'Evolution'

EPITHALAMION, 1934 [1935]
'The Archer'

149

L

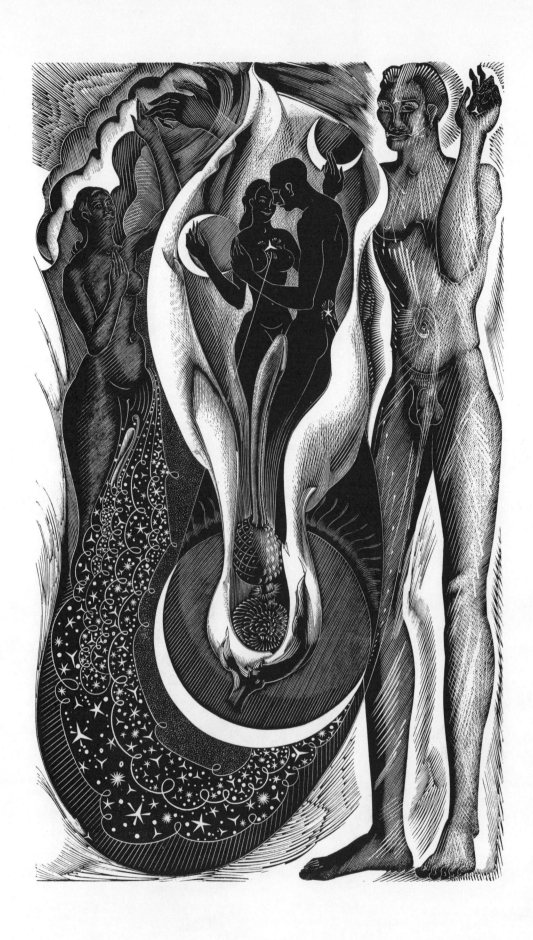

150   EPITHALAMION, 1934 [1935]

'The Bridal'

EPITHALAMION 1934 [1935]   151
'Consummation'

EPITHALAMION, 1934 [1935]
'Perfection'

EPITHALAMION, 1934 [1935]   153
'Fulfilment'

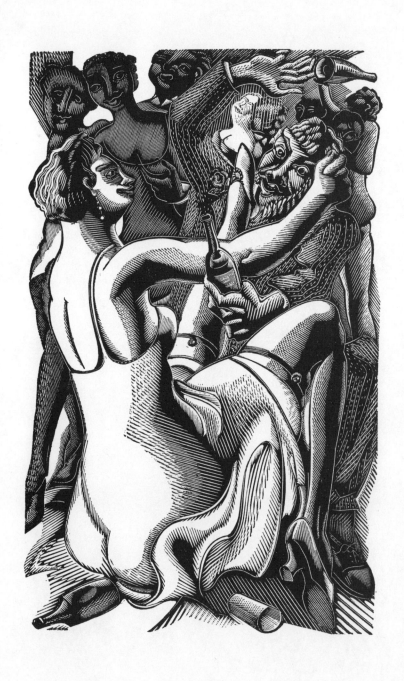

PASTORAL, OR VIRTUE REQUITED, 1935

PASTORAL, OR VIRTUE REQUITED, 1935   155

GWELEDIGAETHEU Y BARDD CWSC, 1940   157
'Saved'

158 MOTHER AND CHILD, [1942]
'Charity' (1934)

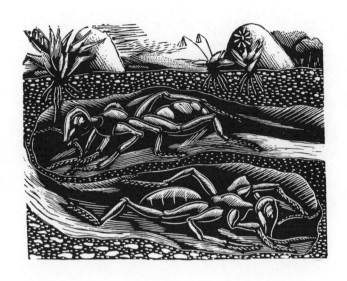

AFRICAN FOLK TALES, 1946   THE . . . OPIUM-EATER, 1948   159
'The Ambitious Ants'   'Pieta' (1930)

160   THE CONFESSIONS OF AN ENGLISH OPIUM-EATER, 1948
'Adolescence' (1930); 'War' (1930)

THE WRECK OF THE GOLDEN MARY, 1956
'Wisdom and Justice'

161

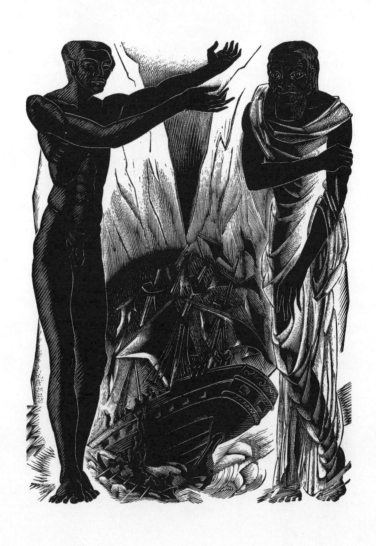

162   THE WRECK OF THE GOLDEN MARY, 1956
'Courage and Temperance'

THE WRECK OF THE GOLDEN MARY, 1956   163
'The Fates'

164 THE BEAST IN THE JUNGLE, 1963

produced by hand
the allen press
md cccc lxx

the book
of genesis
king james bible

THE BOOK OF GENESIS, 1970 (Reduced from 17 × 12½ in)   165

'Problem M', 1924

'Quoits', 1925

M*

'Proud Parents', 1926; 'Lovers', 1926

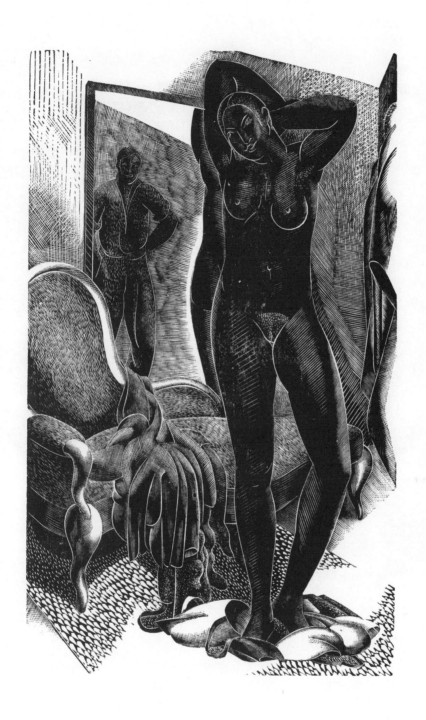

'The Model', 1926

169

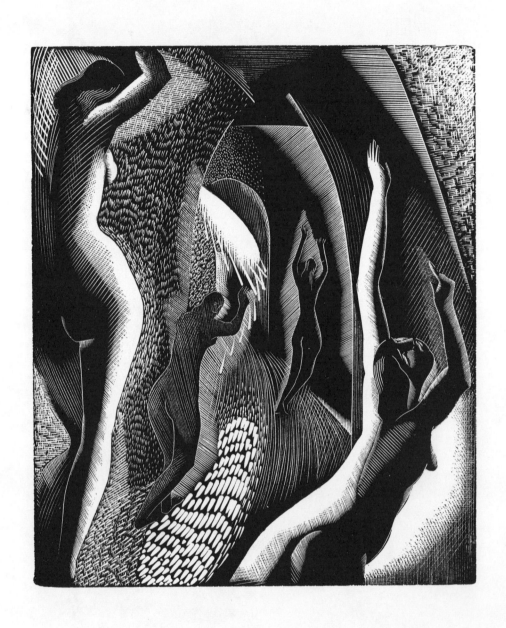

170   'The Maze', 1929

'Emancipation of Woman', 1929   171

'Composition' or 'Holy Family', 1935 ◀
(reduced from 6⅝ × 11 in)

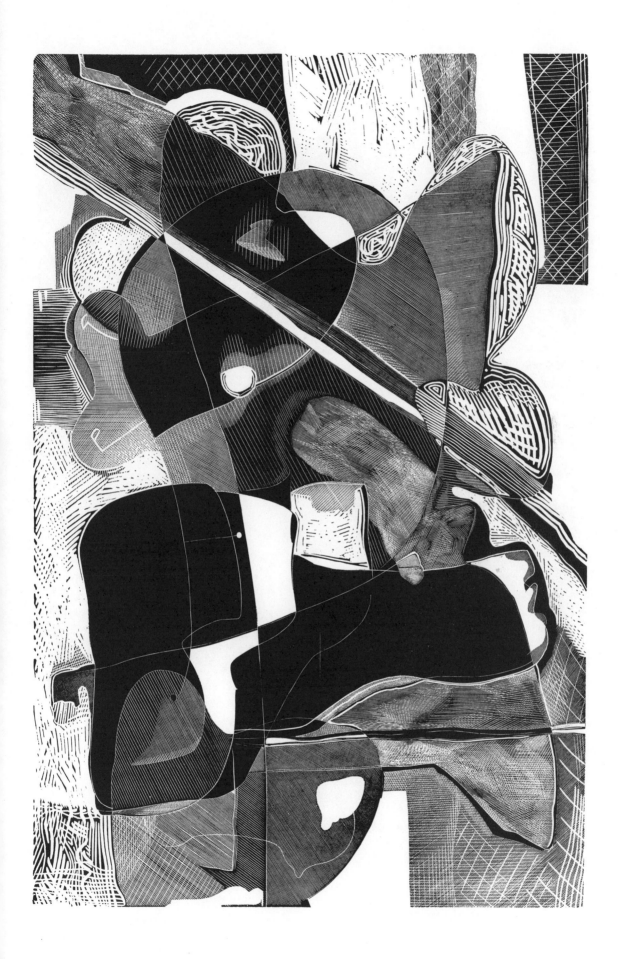

'Composition' or 'Creation', 1936 ◀
(reduced from 8 × 12⅛ in)

174

'Two Figures I', 1937 ◀
(reduced from 9 × 11½ in)

'Figures II', 1937 ◀
(reduced from 9⅛ × 11½ in)

'Venus' or 'Nude', 1938 ◀

INDEX